FOCUSOLOGY

A Breakthrough System for Finding Focus & Achieving Dreams in a Distracted World!

M. Mansoor

Copyright © 2015 by M. Mansoor.

All rights reserved, including the right to reproduce this book or portion thereof in any form whatsoever. No part of this publication may be reproduced without the prior written permission of the publisher, except in the case of brief quotations embodied in critical reviews and certain other noncommercial uses permitted by copyright law.

M. Mansoor/OPX Publishing

Columbia, Maryland

Ordering Information:

Quantity sales: Special discounts are available on quantity purchases by corporations, associations, and others. For details, contact focusology@outlook.com

Focusology / M. Mansoor—2.0 Ed.

ISBN: 978-0-9961754-1-8

Dedicated to those brave souls who commit themselves to changing the world by changing themselves!

"Concentrate all your thoughts upon the work at hand. The sun's rays do not burn until brought to a focus."

—*Alexander Graham Bell*

Table of Contents

FIRST WORDS 7

THE BIG PICTURE 20

THE MACRO FOCUS 41

   THE OBSTACLES 52
      ATTACHMENT TO OUTDATED IDEAS 52
      THE "I LOVE WHAT I DO" ILLUSION 54
      HERD MENTALITY 54
      FEAR OF FAILURE 56
      FEAR OF SUCCESS 56
      LACK OF COURAGE AND MOTIVATION 56
      ENDLESS TALK ABOUT THE UNFAIRNESS 57
      MISCONCEPTIONS ABOUT SMARTNESS 57
      PAST FAILURES 57
   SUGGESTIONS FOR FINDING MACRO FOCUS 59
      KNOW YOURSELF 59
      EXPAND YOUR KNOWLEDGE 60
      TRY PSYCHOMETRIC TESTS 61
      ASK THE RIGHT QUESTIONS 63
      THINK HOLISTIC AND DREAM BIG 64
      IGNORE THE DOUBTERS 65
      CONNECT WITH PEOPLE WHO INSPIRE YOU 66
      TAKE A SABBATICAL 67
      STOP TRYING TO IMPRESS AND START LEARNING 67
      DEVELOP A CREATOR MINDSET 67
      SEE YOURSELF AS YOUR FUTURE SELF 68
      DON'T CHASE TOO MANY RABBITS 68
   ACTIVITIES 69

ACTIVITY: FEELING PROUD 70
ACTIVITY: EMPATHIZING WITH THE OTHER SIDE 71
ACTIVITY: LIFE PURPOSE 72
ACTIVITY: THE WHEEL OF LIFE 73
ACTIVITY: FINDING MACRO FOCUS IN KEY FOCUS AREAS OF
YOUR LIFE 74
ACTIVITY: DRAW DREAM BOARD 76
ACTIVITY: EXPLORING THE MACRO FOCUS 78
ACTIVITY: DISCOVERING CORE VALUES 81

THE MICRO FOCUS 85

THE OBSTACLES 91
  NOT DOING THE PROPER RESEARCH 91
  LACK OF CLARITY 91
  FEAR OF MISSING OUT 91
  PROCRASTINATION 92
  CONSTANT DISTRACTION 92
  NOT UNDERSTANDING THE 'OPPORTUNITY COST' 92
SUGGESTIONS FOR FINDING MICRO FOCUS 94
  START YOUR DAY RIGHT 94
  USE THE 80/20 RULE 96
  CREATE A "TODAY LIST" 97
  CREATE A "TO-BE LIST" 98
  KEEP IT SHORT AND SIMPLE (KISS) 99
  USE THE CREATOR LANGUAGE 99
  CREATE A MONITORING SYSTEM 100
  AVOID DECISION FATIGUE 101
  GO HIGH-TECH 101
  BE GRATEFUL 102
  BE PLAYFUL 103
ACTIVITIES 105

    ACTIVITY: SWOT ANALYSIS 105
    ACTIVITY: FINDING MICRO FOCUS & BUILDING NEW HABITS
    108
    ACTIVITY: WHERE DOES MY TIME GO 112

THE NANO FOCUS 115

The Obstacles 126
    THE ENVIRONMENT 126
    POOR NUTRITION 126
    OVER COMMITMENT 126
    HABIT OF RESPONDING TO EVERYTHING 126
    TOO MUCH WORRYING 127
    MENTAL RESTLESSNESS 127
    PHYSICAL RESTLESSNESS 128

Suggestions for Finding the Nano Focus 129
    HAVE A CLEAR INTENT TO FOCUS 129
    CREATE AN OPTIMAL WORKING ENVIRONMENT 129
    TAKE CARE OF YOUR NUTRITIONAL NEEDS 130
    DON'T DWELL ON THE PAST 130
    PERFORM A RITUAL BEFORE YOU START AN ACTIVITY 131
    DON'T LEAVE TASKS UNFINISHED 132
    FORGIVE, LEARN, FORGET, AND MOVE ON 132
    X-OUT THE WORD FEAR 133
    PLAY GAMES 134
    START REGULAR EXERCISE 134
    FIX THE SOURCE OF YOUR DISTRACTION 135
    TAKE BREAKS 135
    PRACTICE ACTIVE LISTENING 136

Activities 137
    ACTIVITY: COUNTING FORWARD AND BACKWARD 137
    ACTIVITY: DEEP BREATHING 138

ACTIVITY: FULL CONCENTRATION *140*

PUTTING IT ALL TOGETHER **142**

FINAL THOUGHTS **155**

    INDEX 160

    ACKNOWLEDGEMENTS 162

    AUTHOR 163

    PHOTOS ATTRIBUTION 164

    OTHER SELECTED BOOKS BY THE AUTHOR 165

Table of Figures

Figure 1: Focusology 26

Figure 2: Optimal Results 29

Figure 3: Pyramid of Potential 38

Figure 4: The Wheel of Life 73

Figure 5: The DREAM System 146

First Words

FIRST WORDS

It was an early morning of a beautiful fall day in Maryland, USA. I had just gotten to work and after filling my cup with a freshly brewed cup of coffee, I was getting ready for work when my phone bell rang. The guy on the other end of the line seemed really excited to hear my voice. He told me his name and asked if I had recognized him. In my mind, I started going through a list of people with that name and tried to guess if there was a match between the name and the voice, but there was no luck. After a bit of back and forth, and a few minutes of struggle, I finally got it. I felt a little embarrassed for taking so much time to recognize him, but I was happy that after over two decades, I was still able to

FIRST WORDS

do that.

"You have no idea how happy I am to talk to you today," he said in a great excitement.

"I'm very happy to talk to you too," I said with a bit of surprise over what I thought was a bit of an over excitement on his part, as I did not think that we were really that close of friends. As I recalled, he was just a nice kid in the neighborhood, a few years younger than me. I remembered that his father died when he was young. It was just him and his mom. We knew each other well, but we were not close friends.

"You know; I clearly remember the day when I talked to you the last time. And I've been looking for you for all these years," he said. "You probably don't even remember it, but the advice you gave me had completely changed my life."

I certainly did not remember anything, but now I was fully intrigued and wanted to know what he was talking about.

He continued. "The last time we met you were visiting your family after moving out of our hometown to attend a university in another city. At

FIRST WORDS

that time, I had dropped out of college and was totally clueless about what to do next. When you asked me how things were going with me and what I was planning to do next, I did not have much to say. At that time, you sat me down and we talked for over two hours. In those two hours, you gave me the courage to dream again. You convinced me that I needed to restart my studies and make something of myself. You helped me dream and showed me a roadmap to realize my dream. I never saw you after that meeting. After a few months, my family moved to another city and we lost contact. But I've been looking for you ever since. I just wanted to say thank you. I just wanted to tell you that the dream you helped me discover that day changed me forever. I not only finished college, I went on to study journalism in the U.K. and now I've been working as a journalist in a leading British newspaper for many years. I have a great family and I love what I do. Life could not be better."

When he paused after telling his story, I only had a faint recollection of that particular meeting, but I could feel tears in my eyes. I expressed my deep gratitude to him for remembering me and giving me the credit I did not really deserve. I had a great

FIRST WORDS

conversation with him that day and we have stayed in contact ever since.

So, what's the moral of the story?

Simple.

Change is possible.

Now this obviously is not a new discovery. This possibility of change has been the key motivation for teachers and sages both ancient and modern. This is what the latest body of research in fields such as neuroplasticity demonstrates.

We, as humans, have a built-in capacity to change and evolve our beliefs and actions.

We are all capable of making meaningful and positive changes in our lives. We are not destined to be the prisoners of our automated responses. We can choose our thoughts and actions. We don't have to just do things, we can choose where we want to go and then do only what will help us get there, and ignore everything else.

Have you ever tried to change anything about yourself? How was that experience? If you are like most people, your results are not likely to be that great. While change is possible, it's not easy. Creating a New Year Resolution or setting up a goal is never enough; change requires a disciplined approach to self-awareness and self-development. Change is not an event, it's a process.

While it's true that both nature and nurture—how we are born (the genes) and how we are bred or raised (the environment) influence our lives, there is a much larger force in play that ultimately determines our destiny; it's the force of focus. It's what we *choose* to make of ourselves that ultimately determines where we end up in life.

Your genes do not determine your reality; your focus does. If you can harness the power of focus, you can create the reality of your choosing.

Each one of us has something unique to offer to this world. All we truly need is to become aware of it and bring a radical focus to actualizing it. Genes and environmental factors do play a role in shaping human personality, but it's the radical focus on what we choose to become that holds the key to changing destiny.

As humans, we are not different from each other, but

FIRST WORDS

we are not similar either – each one of us is a unique expression of the universe. That uniqueness makes the process of change harder and more exciting, especially if we are talking to about self-directed, sustainable and positive change.

In order for the change to stick, a lot of factors must come together; however, the spark for change happens in an instant, in just one moment. The catalyst for change could be any number of things — a lecture, a movie, a book, a friendly advice, a major life event — that could create a spark for the fire to start, the fire that creates a burning desire in people to be better and do better. Sometimes that spark, that *Aha* moment, is more precious than your entire life. If you ever encounter that, grab it, and allow it to fan the fire that will change your life.

There is a natural desire in all of us to have happier, healthier, and more successful lives. Modern society, enabled by the explosion of information and new ideas, has made it possible for people to have aspirations and dreams that they never had before. People are beginning to believe that they have the right to change and improve all aspects of their lives. They want to improve the experience of their lives.

FIRST WORDS

The age of information is giving way to the age of experience.

The fact of the matter is that everyone and everything in this world are constantly evolving and changing.

Change is the only constant.

No river can be crossed twice. The real challenge is to evolve this natural process of change into a focused and self-guided journey. It's about taking the road that will take you where you need to go, it does not matter if the road is less traveled or frequently traveled. A focused, self-guided change toward a meaningful dream is the freedom that no one should be denied. It's a choice that all human should be able to make.

Awakening, awareness, and the "state of having arrived" are not one-time experiences; they are about an enduring freeing of one's self from limiting dogmas and ideas. These states have nothing to do with achieving a certain amount of wealth, power, fame, or knowledge; they are about a mindset. They are not about reaching a destination, but about discovering a way. They are about arriving at a

FIRST WORDS

mindset of constantly looking for opportunities to grow in every aspect of life. Likewise, the state of transcendence is nothing but transcending your own self and utilizing your skills and abilities to serve others, to make this world a better place for everyone.

After getting a great response for my previous book, *Optimal Xpereince & Art of The FOCUS Method*, which explored a broader system of clearing of and connecting with the inner and outer worlds and living a life based on dreams, values and habits, I felt the need to examine the subject of focus at a deeper level and explore how the power of focus can be employed to be better and do better. The system of *focusology* and this book is the result of that search.

When I searched Google for the phrase "time management" I found 504,000,000 matching results. And when I searched Amazon for "time management" it returned 140,587 matching books. But here is the deal...

Time cannot be managed!

Managing anything requires having a certain degree of control over it, but time is a construct that is

FIRST WORDS

beyond human capacity to even fully understand, forget about controlling and managing it.

What we can do, however, is to choose what we want to pay attention to. In other words, instead of trying to manage time, we should be managing our focus.

In order to *be* or *do* anything worthwhile in life, what we need is to figure out what truly matters, and then bring our optimal focus and concentration to that, and simply forget about the rest.

Meditation, yoga, mindfulness, Zen, and other contemplative practices are great tools for clearing the mind. The desired outcome of these practices is to gain calmness and composure—nothing more, nothing less. It's about clearing the soil from weeds and preparing it for the seeds.

Focusology is not meditation; it's a state beyond. Focusology is about sowing the seeds and nurturing them when the soil has been cleared of the weeds. It's about discovering and pursuing what truly matters and ignoring everything else. In other words, Focusology is *mindfulness with a purpose*.

Meditation is a therapy that helps alleviate the suffering; Focusology is a strategy that helps

FIRST WORDS

optimize the living. The therapy should not be confused with the strategy. Therapy has its place in finding calm and serenity in the crazy world we live in, but make no mistake, success is not measured by how much suffering we manage to avoid; it is measured by how much imagination, courage, and discipline we manage to muster to pursue what is meaningful.

The system of Focusology is developed as a transformational tool that brings together lessons from ancient and modern wisdom traditions as well as the latest scientific research from various disciplines.

This book presents a holistic yet radically simple way to discover what truly matters in life, and shares some time-tested and science-based tools to do the most important things with optimal focus and concentration.

There is way too much confusion in the field of personal development and self-help. There are layers of vested interests that profit from this complexity. My intention here is not to get bogged down by complex ideas and theories; I want to make things radically simple and actionable. My intention

FIRST WORDS

here is to make ideas easily understandable and usable. This book is intended to help you find focus in a world that is full of hocus pocus.

Focus matters, because a successful person is an ordinary person with an extraordinary focus.

There is nothing mysterious about success; success is a natural outcome of following a system that leads to success.

Focusology is a system that will help you harness the power of focus in order to optimize performance and achieve success in every aspect of life. Focusology is not tied to any one method of knowledge and discovery; it's an interdisciplinary approach that lives at the nexus of applied anthropology, positive psychology, and philosophy.

It's a system that brings it all together for anyone who yearns for finding focus and achieving dreams in a distracted world.

CHAPTER ONE

The Big Picture

WHAT IS IT ALL ABOUT?

THE BIG PICTURE

"A scholar knows many books; a well-educated person has knowledge and skills; an enlightened person understands the meaning and purpose of his life...The only real science is the knowledge of how a person should live his life. And this knowledge is open to everyone."

– Leo Tolstoy

Ever wonder why some people seem to succeed in everything they do on a consistent basis while many others don't get anywhere no matter how hard they try? It seems that

THE BIG PICTURE

everything that these successful people touch turns into gold; they seem happier, healthier, and wealthier in every aspect of their lives. Although it's very tempting to simply attribute their success to things like luck, kismet, karma, or coincidence; the empirical evidence seems to point to something different, something that we have a lot of control over.

Allow me to explain.

It is true that there are always certain factors that are beyond individual control that could affect outcomes in life, but there is no disputing the fact that if we choose to focus on what we *can* control, our outcomes will be far different than those who leave things to chance. It is my belief that success does not happen by chance, it happens by choice. We succeed when our actions are driven by a clear intention to succeed.

Success is not an event, it's a *system*.

It's a system that we can learn and apply to bring meaningful and measurable changes to every aspect of our lives. We can survive and make a living by learning some marketable skills, but if we intend to

THE BIG PICTURE

thrive and achieve extraordinary success, we must build a system.

If you study the lives of successful people, you will notice that there are certain key habits that distinguish them from the rest of the pack:

> *"All that we are is the result of what we have thought."*
>
> *– Buddha*

1. They have a clear sense of direction in terms of what they want to *be, do,* and *achieve*.
2. They are constantly looking for better ways of getting to their destination.
3. They know the art of being in the present moment and bringing full attention to the task at hand, on a consistent basis.

According to a University of Scranton study, only 8% of people actually achieve their New Year's resolutions—which means a whopping 92% of the people fail to achieve what they set out to do. These people want to change and succeed; these are well-intentioned people with a vision for a better tomorrow, but only 8% of them succeed. This is startling.

THE BIG PICTURE

So what's going here? I believe that primarily there are three reasons why most people fail to achieve their goals:

- Their goals are reductionist, uninspiring or negative.

> "I once asked a bird, how is it that you fly in this gravity of darkness?
>
> The bird responded, 'Love lifts me.'"
>
> – Hāfez

- They fail to accurately identify and do what is required to achieve their goals.
- They are not able to pay full attention to the task at hand, on a consistent basis.

Fact of the matter is, if you want to increase your chances of achieving success in any aspect of your life, goals are simply not enough, you need a *system* — a structure and methodology that is holistic, simple and effective. A system that helps you to:

1. Evolve your goals to a holistic, positive, and inspiring vision/dream.
2. Discover and commit to what needs to be done on a daily basis to achieve the

THE BIG PICTURE

vision/dream.

3. Learn the art of mindfulness to do those things with optimal focus.

I call this system *Focusology*.

What is Focusology?

Focusology is a disciplined pursuit of what is meaningful.

The system consists of three modules which cover the three things that a person has to get right to achieve true and meaningful success:

1. Macro Focus (*Why*): intention, vision, dream
2. Micro Focus (*What*): action, daily routines, habits
3. Nano Focus (*How*): attention, mindfulness, being in the present moment

Here is graphical representation of the idea:

THE BIG PICTURE

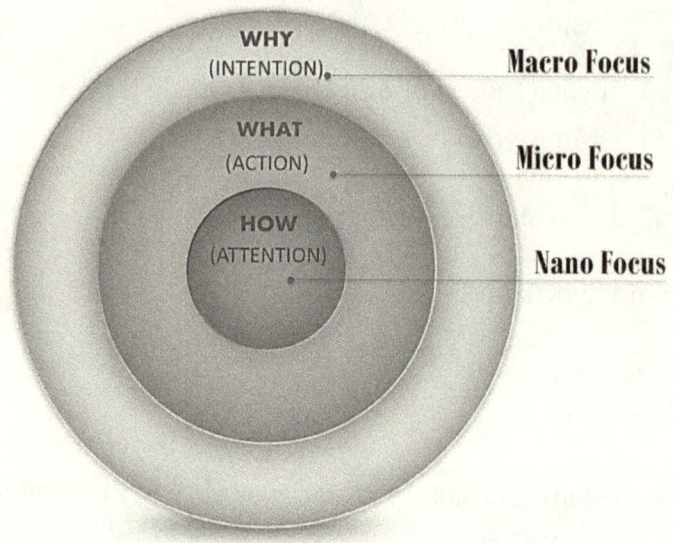

Figure 1: Focusology

Macro Focus is about *why* and intention. It's about discovering your vision and mission in life. It's about finding a purpose and dreaming a dream. It's the intention that drives daily actions. It's a meaningful dream that helps you find your True North. Many people spend their lives fighting the old, not realizing that true greatness can only be realized by finding the new and being laser focused on actualizing it. Being poor have nothing to do with the lack of money; it's the lack of a dream that makes people poor.

Micro Focus is *what* needs to be done on a daily basis

THE BIG PICTURE

to achieve your Macro Focus. These are the actions you need to take—your daily routines and habits. When tied to a larger vision, these small steps make a huge difference,

> *"Each morning we are born again. What we do today is what matters most."*
>
> — Buddha

but random small steps without any Marco Focus rarely lead to any meaningful change.

What Micro Focus does is that it shifts the uncertainty of a future into a measurable activity of today.

1. Your dream of becoming a successful lawyer five years from now shifts into a measurable activity of time spent studying today.

2. Your dream of living a long and healthy life shifts into a measurable activity of a number of steps walked today.

3. Your dream of becoming an author shifts into a measurable activity of a number of words written today.

In short, Micro Focus generates instant gratification

THE BIG PICTURE

through measurement of activities that are coordinated for the delayed gratification of future dreams. This matters as we need to feel good about us today as we pursue our long-term dreams.

Nano Focus is about learning *how* you actually do your tasks. It's about bringing your full attention to the task at hand. It's about being in the present moment without any judgment. Resistance creates persistence; the path to transformation goes through the acceptance of the way things are.

All three levels of focus are tightly inter-connected. Those who stick to one but ignore the other do so at their own peril. The *why* (intention), the *what* (action), and the *how* (attention) must all come together to produce optimal results. An *intention* without *action* is hallucination, and an *action* without *attention* is self-deception.

After you find these three levels of focus, everything will start falling into place. A doorway to a life of optimal experiences will be opened for you. Old habits die hard. In the beginning, development of such a system may not be easy, but as soon as you get going, it gets easy. Swimming turns into floating. Instead of fighting the waves, you learn to leverage

THE BIG PICTURE

them to your advantage. You realize that headwinds are not obstacles; they are there to help you fly higher. What you might have considered a failure in the past turns into learning, which only helps you to refine your approach.

As depicted in the following illustration, optimal results can only be found at the intersection of right intention, right action, and right attention.

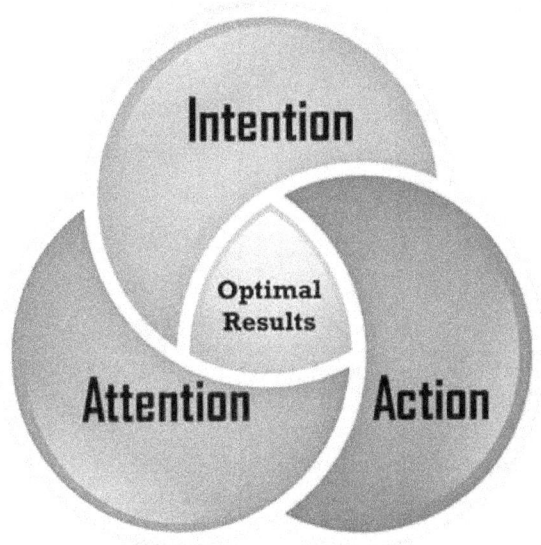

Figure 2: Optimal Results

If any of these three ingredients are out of alignment, your results and your experience cannot be optimal. This process and criteria apply every time to

THE BIG PICTURE

everything you do; without it, you run the risk of losing your sense of destination, getting involved in activities that don't help move you closer to your destination, or doing things without the attention that is needed.

Let's look at the following table to see how focused and non-focused people think and act differently.

NON-FOCUSED	FOCUSED
Macro Focus (INTENTION, WHY)	
• Driven by what is popular • Unaware of their strengths & weaknesses • Motivated by the need to impress others	• Driven by their own dreams and goals • Aware of their strengths and weaknesses • Motivated by the need to learn & grow
Micro Focus (ACTION, WHAT)	
• Oblivious to how their daily actions contribute to their dreams • Easily distracted by everything that comes their way • Lack the discipline to measure their progress	• Ensure their daily actions are in alignment with their dreams • Steadfast in completing their predetermined tasks • Constantly measure their progress

THE BIG PICTURE

Nano Focus (ATTENTION, HOW)	
• Cherish busyness & commotion • Keep their space messy & cluttered • Believe multi-tasking can help them do more things	• Nurture awareness & concentration • Keep their space clear & uncluttered • Believe uni-tasking can help them do things better

As you can see, there is a very clear distinction between those who harness the power of focus and those who are oblivious to it. This distinction ultimately leads to entirely different results for these two groups of people. Those who commit to optimizing their life by refining their Macro, Micro and Nano focuses not only actualize their dreams but also discover that real joy is found in the journey.

The *way* is the *destination*!

In a way, life is like Google: if you search for "life sucks" on Google, you are going to find millions of matches, and if you really start reading them, you will have no trouble justifying why your life really sucks. But if you search for "life is great," you are sure to fund countless matches and reasons for that too. Like Google, the universe just returns to you what you are searching for. If you are searching for misery, gloom, and evil, you are certainly going to find plenty of it, but if your search is for joy, bliss, and good, that's exactly what you are likely to find. The key is to learn to ask the right questions. Instead of asking, "How can I survive?" you can ask, "How can I thrive?" and you will be surprised to see how it changes everything. What you get back from the universe always depends on what you ask for.

The system of Focusology is designed to help you look for and focus on what works well and what is positive in life. Focusology is different from traditional approaches to change. It does not start with the identification of a problem that needs fixing; it starts with the discovery of a meaningful dream that merits actualizing. Most traditional approaches to change and self-development are problem or deficiency-focused. They are meant to eliminate the suffering. These approaches focus on current needs and look for reductionist solutions with a win-lose mindset. Focusology looks for and builds on strengths. It is relationship-based, outcome-driven approach to sustainable change.

Let's look at the chart to compare the traditional approaches with Focusology.

THE BIG PICTURE

TRADITIONAL APPROACHES	FOCUSOLOGY
• Identify a problem	• Discover a meaningful dream/vision.
• Analyze the causes	• Recognize what already works well
• Identify possible solutions	• Establish new habits & routines
• Implement the plan to solve the problem	• Accurately measure the progress & adjust the course as needed

Our reality is created by what we choose to focus on. When we focus on problems, the best we can do is to identify the causes of what is broken and try not to do those things in the future. However, the moment we shift our focus from problems to opportunities, and from what we want to avoid to what we want to *be*, our whole world changes, and our new focus starts creating our new reality.

Who we are as humans is not a static occurrence; we are an emergent phenomenon, we are creating ourselves every moment through our thoughts, words, and actions. What is needed is a shift in focus. Instead of seeing ourselves, and the world around

THE BIG PICTURE

us, as a problem that needs a solution, we need to learn to see the opportunities; we need to see the potential. And that's what the system of Focusology is designed for. It's not a toolkit for solving problems; it's a meditation on human potential.

Failure is the inability to dream your own dreams. And success is having meaningful dreams and the courage to follow through. When you follow your meaningful dreams with a focused plan, there is no failure; there is only growth. The system proposed in this book will exponentially increase your chances of realizing your dreams, but even when dreams are not realized in the timeframe or the manner in which you expect them to come true, you learn that the real joy is the experience. You learn that the true secret of life is that it's really about the journey, not the destination.

It's like eating a delicious meal: your objective is not to finish it as fast as you can so that you can check off another activity from your to-do list. You actually slow down to enjoy every bite of it and wish that the food would not end too soon. That's exactly what happens when you are pursuing meaningful dreams: the journey becomes so exhilarating that reaching the destination becomes secondary. Your job is to simply follow the road because road knows the way.

The challenge most people face is that they never become aware of their subconscious behavior

THE BIG PICTURE

patterns and never realize their true potential. They simply don't know what they don't know. They live their lives in a state of self-apathy and unawareness. However, all of us do have the potential to change and grow from that state of self-

> *It's your road and yours alone. Others may walk it with you, but no one can walk it for you.*
>
> *– Rumi*

apathy and become more self-aware. There are two fundamental desires that could drive this change: the desire to avoid the pain of an existing situation and the desire to seek the pleasure of potential outcomes.

Self-awareness is a stage when people start connecting with their deeper selves. They develop a sharp capacity to understand their own personalities, including their strengths, weakness, desires, dreams, aspirations, values, and beliefs. Once they become self-aware, they start seeing the potential for change and growth that exists in each one of us.

Self-awareness ultimately leads to self-development. Self- development is a disciplined pursuit of change and growth in all aspects of life — physical, social,

THE BIG PICTURE

emotional, mental, and spiritual. In this stage, people start focusing on improving various aspects of their lives. They start going after what they want instead of just waiting for the good things to happen. Instead of sitting in a passenger seat, they decide to take control of the steering wheel of their lives. The

> *When "I" was then He was not, now, He "is" and "I" am not*
>
> *All the darkness mitigated, when I saw the light within.*
>
> *— Kabir. An Indian Mystic*

choose to become CEOs of their own lives.

After people taste the sweet nectar of success and start enjoying the benefits of self-development, they want to share it with others. They start seeing the unrealized potential in others and want to help them in their journey from self-apathy to self-awareness and self- development.

This final stage is called self-transcendence. In this stage, people are able to transcend their own self, and help others in their journey. This is a state where people rise above their own interests and share their talents to make this world a better place for everyone. Different traditions have different names

THE BIG PICTURE

for this state. Self-realization, non-dualism, *Fina*, Jivanmukti, and *Nirvana* are all great ways to describe this final stage where self dissolves into the ultimate reality and a person starts seeing the unity and oneness in all that exists.

Let's look at the following picture and table to understand the full spectrum of change and growth, and see how Focusology relates to potential of human evolution from self-apathy to self-transcendence.

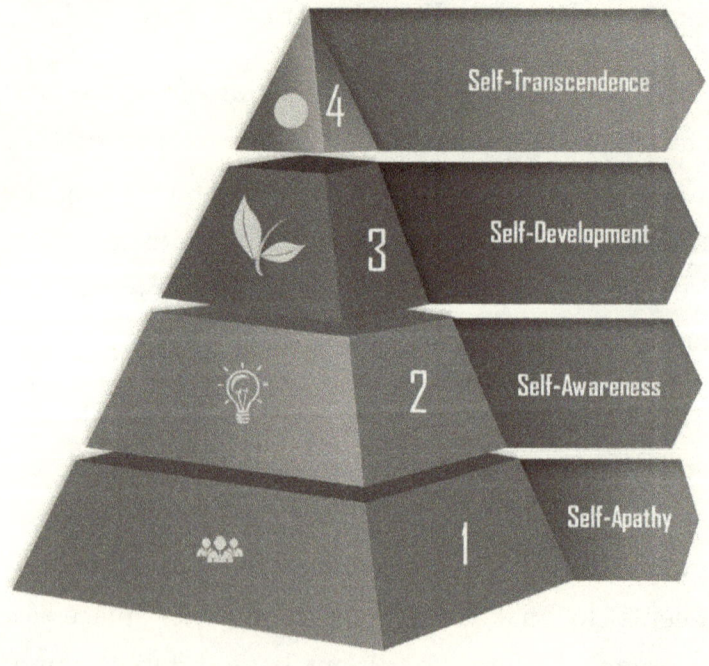

Figure 3: Pyramid of Potential

THE BIG PICTURE

Here is the breakdown of key characteristic people generally exhibit during each of these stages. To better understand it, try reading the table from the bottom.

STAGE	CHARACTERISTICS
4- Self-Transcendence	• Practice gratefulness • Actively seek opportunities to give back • Work toward leaving a positive legacy
3- Self-Development	• Know their goals/dreams and focus on achieving them • Take consistent action and nurture mindfulness • Seek feedback & learn from their actions
2- Self-Awareness	• Aware of their strengths & weaknesses • Seek to change and invite feedback • Start learning from their failures and mistakes
1- Self-Apathy	• Unaware of their strengths & weaknesses • Stick with traditions & resist feedback • Hide mistakes and failures

This journey from self-apathy to self-transcendence is the most natural path a human being can travel, but so many people get stuck in the abyss of self-apathy because of social conditioning. People who

THE BIG PICTURE

have the potential but never realize it are like acorns that degenerate without ever becoming oak trees. A degenerated oak seed is a wasted potential; a fully grown oak tree gives back to the nature that brought it into existence.

This book is not meant to be a philosophical mambo jumbo meant for intellectual enticement; it's a practical guide for those who want to find focus and achieve their dreams. It is my hope that this book will give you a better sense of self-awareness and introduce you to useful ideas and tools that can assist you as you continue your journey toward self-transcendence.

CHAPTER TWO

The Macro Focus

DISCOVERING A MEANINGFUL DREAM

THE MACRO FOCUS

"You will not do incredible things without an incredible dream."

– John Eliot

The Macro Focus is the first module of the Focusology system. Macro Focus is about finding and focusing on what truly matters in life. It's also known by words such as *Calling*, *Passion*, and *True North*. It's that one thing that you feel passionate about. It's the driving force that gets you

THE MACRO FOCUS

out of the bed every morning and gives you the energy and drive to go through the day. It's that secret ingredient that adds zest, and flavor to your life. Macro Focus is your connection to something

> *"Out beyond ideas of wrong-doing, and right-doing there is a field.*
> *I'll meet you there."*
> *– Rumi*

that is larger than yourself. It's the *why* that helps you choose a way.

Many people struggle through life because instead of focusing on what they want, they focus on what they *don't* want. They get into the habit of thinking and talking about everything that they perceive to be wrong in their world. If you listen to their stories carefully, you will notice that they always play the role of a victim. Blaming the world becomes their way of justifying their shortcomings.

On the other hand, focused people dedicate their energies to what they *do* want. They like to think and talk about the potential and possibilities. It's not that they are ignorant about the challenges and hurdles; they, in fact, are very mindful and realistic people. They just develop an uncanny ability to identify

THE MACRO FOCUS

potential in themselves and others. They can see an oak tree in an acorn, with full realization that the journey from the seed to the tree will not be easy. The seed is going to need water, sunshine, protection, and nurturing in order for it to mature into a tree. But they know that potential is there. They are aware of the risks, but they are willing to take their chances.

> *"The mystery of human existence lies not in just staying alive, but in finding something to live for."*
>
> *– Fyodor Dostoyevsky, The Brothers Karamazov*

For some people, finding Macro Focus is easy. They just feel it inside and know what they want from their lives; for many others, it's an elusive and evolving concept. It could take many different forms as people go through different phases of life. Whether your Macro Focus is to change the world or just to be happy and share happiness with whoever you meet, the key is to never forget it. And always make it the reason behind all your decisions.

Macro Focus is not necessarily a static construct. It's really a gradual unfolding of one's true being. There

THE MACRO FOCUS

are mountains beyond mountains, but you don't really see what's next until you've climbed the first mountain. Each peak is a start of a new journey. It's really the journey that you are seeking. It's about the process. Your job is to optimize the process; the outcome will take care of itself. Sometimes a student may not be able to see all the possibilities that lie ahead until he finishes his degree, and that's OK; he has to climb the first mountain before new vistas are revealed to him.

Taking care of family, holding a steady job, and meeting social obligations are very noble things and require a great degree of discipline and commitment, however, Macro Focus is bigger than all of these things; Macro Focus is about optimizing all facets of life, and then using one's mental and physical energies in the service of something larger than one's own self. All the progress in the world has been made possible by people who found their purpose and had the courage and discipline to pursue it. These are the people who had the wisdom to see beyond tradition and dogma, and courage to put their hearts and souls into achieving a meaningful dream.

THE MACRO FOCUS

Most people would say that they have a general idea of what they want from life and what their Macro Focus is. But in most cases, they are just guessing. There is a difference between guessing and knowing. Knowing involves clarity and commitment, knowing leads to action. However, guessing is just an effort to avoid being perceived as clueless. It's just self-deception.

Macro Focus is not just about figuring out what you like and doing that for the rest of your life. It's about stretching your self-perceived limits. The fact of the matter is that life without challenge is not worth living. The real fun of life lies in getting out of your comfort zone. Comfort zones are, well, comfortable, but the problem with them is that they do not help you grow. They are a barren land. In order to grow, you must get out of your comfort zone and test your limits.

In order to find out what you are made of, you must get over the self-imposed limitations and dare to dream things that you thought were beyond you. Your fears, trepidations, phobias, and apprehensions reside in your own head. Your perception is not reality. It's your understanding of the reality. It's

THE MACRO FOCUS

your perspective, but it's not the reality. And if you are daring enough to evolve your understanding, and your reality will change.

> *"He who says he can and he who says he can't, are both usually right."*
>
> *— Confucius*

Your reality is simply your *interpretation* of reality that is based on your past experiences—both positive and negative. After you understand that basic truth about reality, you can begin to become aware of your fixed and deep-seated ways of thinking, feeling and behaving. It is that awareness that provides the understanding of things that don't really matter. It also gives you a better understanding of what should really matter.

In a way, life is absurd. And that very fact creates a great challenge as well as a great opportunity for each one of us. It's a challenge because life can appear futile and meaningless in many aspects. It's also an opportunity because we have the power to assign it a meaning that works for us. If we can free ourselves of socially conditioned and preconceived interpretations of reality and success, we can begin to discover our own unique talents, gifts, strengths, and innate abilities. The ultimate meaning of life is

THE MACRO FOCUS

to groom our unique talents and gifts and use them to the service of humanity.

> *"What you seek is seeking you."*
>
> *– Rumi*

In short, knowing your *why* is the first step to any sustainable change. Purpose, passion, meaning, mission, cause, goal, intention or belief — anything that inspires you to take the right action — is a good name for Macro Focus. The key is to remember that without finding your *why*, the *Macro Focus*, there is no change, and there is no progress. What is the point of climbing a ladder that is leaning against the wrong wall? Climbing such a ladder does involve effort, but every step you take will only take you away from where you need to be. So, before you start climbing the ladder of life, make sure it's leaning against the right wall. Before you start doing the things right, you must make sure you are doing the right things.

What Macro Focus helps you do is to create something in your mind that does not exist yet. The Macro Focus is your vivid imagination — a clear mental picture — of a future that is better than your present reality. Like a car's GPS, it provides you turn

THE MACRO FOCUS

by turn directions and helps you figure out if your actions are helping you move toward your destination or away from it. Without a clear Macro Focus, you will ultimately find yourself drifting aimlessly in the treacherous sea of life.

> *"Be the change that you wish to see in the world."*
>
> *— Mahatma Gandhi*

When you find your Macro Focus, here are some of the wonderful things that would begin to happen:

- You get motivated. Your willpower is limited. When the going gets tough, you need a meaningful, positive and holistic dream to keep pushing.

- Your actions become measurable. Progress is not just doing things; progress is doing things that help you move closer to your goal. A clearly stated Macro Focus makes your actions measurable and meaningful.

- You get a clearer sense of direction. You get a standard against which you can measure your decisions. There are junctions in life where having a clear sense of your direction will help you say no to things that don't help

THE MACRO FOCUS

you move toward your destination.

- Instead of complaining about what's wrong in your life, you become focused on a plan to fix it. You evolve from problem mindset to solution mindset. This matters because what you choose to focus on will expand. Shifting your focus to what you want will help attract the resources you need to actualize it.

- You become mindful of the resources you already have — people and things that could help you achieve your goal.

- Instead of comparing yourself with others, you start comparing yourself to your yesterday's self. Instead of feeling bad about not comparing too well with others, you start feeling good about being better than where you were yesterday. As a focused person, you are motivated by the desire to achieve your own vision, not by the desire to be better than others.

- After you find your Macro Focus, you start defining yourself by your desired future state, not by your past or even present.

- You discover your real community. Your

THE MACRO FOCUS

community is not just the people who you know through your work and social circle; your real community is your fellow travelers. They are the people with similar goals and aspirations in life.

> "You were born with wings, why prefer to crawl through life?"
>
> – Rumi

Finding the Macro Focus could be magical. Why, then, do so many people keep drifting in life without ever figuring out where they are going?

In the following section, let's discuss some of the most common obstacles people face in finding their Macro Focus.

THE MACRO FOCUS

The Obstacles

The pace and complexity of modern life is so crazy that it's very easy to get lost and lose track of what truly matters. Mundane details of life can easily consume all the hours we have in a day, leaving no time to slow down, reflect, and get a meaningful perspective on life.

Here are some of the common challenges people encounter when it comes to finding the Macro Focus.

ATTACHMENT TO OUTDATED IDEAS

Ideas don't come with expiration dates but maybe they should, because even the best ideas can only be useful for a certain situation at a certain time. Change is the only constant in this world. We change as we grow old and so does everything around us. We constantly need new ideas to respond to the ever-changing world. In order to make room for the new ideas, old ones must be purged on a regular basis. Some people get too attached to the ideas instead of keeping the focus on the outcomes and being attached to the process that creates those outcomes.

Sometimes the real challenge is not how to acquire

THE MACRO FOCUS

more, it's how to let go of what we have gotten used to, how to unlearn and X-out what no longer serves any purpose. It's like stripping the old paint before new paint could be applied. In order for new to stick, old must be stripped. Ask any painter, and he will tell you that stripping the old paint is a lot harder than applying the fresh one.

You might have heard the story of a university professor who went to visit a famous master on the mountaintop to seek some answers. Having spent his entire life in learning and teaching, the professor was very proud of his accomplishments. While the master quietly served tea, the professor talked about his knowledge and wisdom. The master poured the visitor's cup to the brim, and then he kept pouring. The professor watched the overflowing cup until he could no longer restrain himself.

"It's over full! No more will go in!" the professor blurted.

"You are like this cup," the master replied. "How can you learn anything if your mind is already full?"

Change is only possible if we are willing to empty our cups. Here is how the great Russian sage, Leo

THE MACRO FOCUS

Tolstoy, puts it;

> *"It is better to know less than necessary than to know more than necessary. Do not fear the lack of knowledge, but truly fear unnecessary knowledge which is acquired only to please vanity."*

THE "I LOVE WHAT I DO" ILLUSION

Sometimes people just can't let go of the situation they are in. They convince themselves that they like what they do, but deep inside their hearts they know the truth. They know that there is more to life than the aimlessness of the rat race they claim to love.

HERD MENTALITY

Many people undervalue the importance of finding their own Macro Focus because of social influence and herd mentality. They adopt the ideals and dreams of the group they identify with as their own. In this deindividuation process, they lose a sense of their own self.

THE MACRO FOCUS

Some people just want to do what *everyone* around them seems to be doing. Based on people's group, tribe, creed, ethnicity, language and nationality, the definition of *everyone* changes, but what this obstacle really amounts

> "Run my dear,
> From anything
> That may not strengthen
> Your precious budding wings."
>
> – Hāfez

to is people's willingness to give up their right to choose their own destiny. They tend to believe that their life's purpose, their Macro Focus, is somehow pre-determined based on their association to a certain group.

John Maynard Keynes, a celebrated British economist, made the following observation on the dangers of herd mentality in his famous work *The General Theory of Employment, Interest, and Money*:

> "Worldly wisdom teaches that it is better for reputation to fail conventionally than to succeed unconventionally."

THE MACRO FOCUS

FEAR OF FAILURE

Sometimes people know what they want but keep it hidden inside because they are afraid of failing. They are not confident that they have what it takes to achieve their dreams.

FEAR OF SUCCESS

As crazy as it may appear, there are people who are afraid of being successful. They feel that hiding their talents, keeping their head low, and not getting noticed is a safe bet. They don't want to face the unknown even when they know the enormous potential it holds.

> *"Let the young soul survey its own life with a view of the following question: What have you truly loved thus far? What has ever uplifted your soul, what has dominated and delighted it at the same time?"*
>
> *— Nietzsche*

LACK OF COURAGE AND MOTIVATION

Some people overestimate the effort it takes to pursue their dreams. They come up with all sorts of excuses: "I am too old for this", "I don't have time", and "I've too many responsibilities" and more.

THE MACRO FOCUS

ENDLESS TALK ABOUT THE UNFAIRNESS

Acquiring knowledge about how the world works is awesome; using that knowledge as an excuse for not taking action is awful. The world works the way it works. Calling the world unfair does not change anything. Instead of developing a vision for a better tomorrow and taking action to actualize it, some people get into the habit of endlessly talking about their self-perceived unfairness of the world.

MISCONCEPTIONS ABOUT SMARTNESS

Hard work and consistency beat smartness every time, yet so many people don't dream big because they don't score well against the socially and academically accepted criteria for smartness. They fail to appreciate the value of having a clear target and courage to work hard consistently, no matter where they stand today.

PAST FAILURES

Past experiences are another set of obstacles that keep people from finding their Macro Focus. Instead of learning from their past experiences and using them as growth opportunities, they use them as a validation of not being good enough to try

THE MACRO FOCUS

something big in life.

THE MACRO FOCUS

Suggestions for Finding Macro Focus

Now that we have talked about what is keeping us from finding our Macro Focus, let's look at some of the ways to overcome above-mentioned obstacles and find a way through endless distractions life throws at us.

KNOW YOURSELF

You can only transform what you understand. The process of transformation starts with understanding your true self or gaining self-awareness, and self-awareness results from contemplation, meditation, and philosophical self-reflection. This is how Confucius describes this concept:

> "By three methods we may learn wisdom: First, by reflection, which is noblest; second, by imitation, which is easiest; and third by experience, which is the bitterest."

This self-awareness should help you gain a deeper understanding of your values, beliefs, and

THE MACRO FOCUS

philosophy. Success is an inside job. If you want to be different, you must think differently.

> *"There is a voice that doesn't use words. Listen."*
>
> *– Rumi*

Your future is a manifestation of how you see yourself today. You don't have to see yourself as an outcome of your past; see yourself as potential that the future holds. You are not where you are coming from; you are where you want to be. You don't drive your car by looking into the rearview mirror, so why drive life that way?

EXPAND YOUR KNOWLEDGE

Before you can learn something deep and narrow, you need to go wide and shallow. Read, watch, and learn about a variety of subjects. Develop at least a foundational understanding of subjects such as psychology, anthropology, history, philosophy, physics, chemistry, biology, computer sciences, etc. This will help you connect the dots and see the forest for the trees. This will help you develop a *systems approach* to thinking and solving problems.

THE MACRO FOCUS

TRY PSYCHOMETRIC TESTS

Modern personality/psychometric tests and inventories have come a long way since their humble beginnings in the early twentieth century when they were first used for recruitment in the armed forces. Personality tests can help reveal an individual's psychological makeup and suggest ways to address areas of concern. Some of the most popular tests and inventories are:

- **Myers-Briggs Type Indicator (MBTI):** A useful tool for understanding psychological preferences in how people perceive the world and make decisions

- **Minnesota Multiphasic Personality Inventory (MMPI):** The most widely used tool to assess personality traits and psychopathology.

- **Fundamental Interpersonal Relations Orientation (FIRO):** A tool and theory of personal assessment for improving interpersonal relations and personal effectiveness.

THE MACRO FOCUS

- **Social Styles Assessment:** A simple and practical tool for self-awareness interpersonal effectiveness

> *"Every generation needs a new revolution."*
>
> — *Thomas Jefferson*

- **DiSC (Drive, Influence, Steadiness, Compliance) Assessment:** A personal and team assessment tool for improving relationships, teamwork, and communication.

- **Five-Factor Model:** This is not a test but a model that looks at the five main features of human personality: Openness, Conscientiousness, Extraversion, Agreeableness, and Neuroticism.

This field of psychology is still evolving, and no psychometric test/assessment tool can truly capture the richness of human personality. However, any of these tests/assessment tools can put you in the mindset of looking inside yourself and reflecting. These tests/assessment tools can also help you understand the similarities and differences among

THE MACRO FOCUS

people.

ASK THE RIGHT QUESTIONS

Self-awareness is not about having all the answers; it's a matter of asking the right questions. Here are some key questions you can ask yourself to begin your journey of finding your Marco Focus:

> *"Come, seek, for search is the foundation of fortune: every success depends upon focusing the heart."*
>
> *– Rumi*

- Who am I?
- What are my core values?
- What are my priorities?
- What strengths and weakness do I have?
- What kind of legacy do I want to leave behind?
- How do I want to be remembered after I die?

Finding Macro Focus requires that you undertake an inward journey. It requires going inside. It comes from contemplation, introspection, and self-reflection. It requires qualities such as humility, integrity, courage, commitment, passion, confidence, creativity, and fairness. It requires

THE MACRO FOCUS

asking yourself the right questions and having the audacity to let your own answers lead the way for a new and better life.

> *"Without the playing with fantasy no creative work has ever yet come to birth. The debt we owe to the play of imagination is incalculable."*
>
> *– Carl Jung*

THINK HOLISTIC AND DREAM BIG

The challenge many people face is that they try to apply reductionist approaches to understanding and solving holistic problems. They are trying to fix the whole by changing a small part.

They are like those six blind men who went to "see" an elephant and got into an argument about what the elephant looked like. The man who touched the tail of the elephant argued that it looked like a rope. The man who touched its leg thought that elephant was like a pillar. The one who touched the trunk claimed that the elephant was like a tree branch. The one who felt the elephant's ear claimed that it was like a huge hand-fan. The man who felt the belly of the elephant stressed that elephant was really like a wall. And the one who touched the tusk of the elephant was sure that it was like a solid pipe.

THE MACRO FOCUS

Everyone thought that they were right. They started arguing and got agitated. Finally, a passerby saw what was going on, and settled the issue by explaining to them that they were all right, as the elephant had all of those features, but in order for them to fully understand the elephant — as a whole — they needed to combine their understanding and create a holistic picture of the elephant.

You must create a holistic understanding of the issues and then address these issues from a holistic perspective.

Don't base your dreams on where you have come from or even on where you stand now. See the potential and imagine a future that is bigger and better than any limitation of your current situation. If the dream is not big, it will lack the power to inspire you. The Placebo Effect is real, and Murphy's Law is only a myth. Go ahead and dream big.

IGNORE THE DOUBTERS

No matter what your dream is, there will always be people who will doubt them. They will point out all

THE MACRO FOCUS

the reasons why you are crazy to even think about your dream. These are people who can find problem to every solution. Fact of the matter is, no matter how hard you try, not everyone is going to like you or believe in you. And it has nothing to do with you or your dream; that's just the way some people are. It's not your job to change them, and to make them like you; your job is to focus on your dreams and simply ignore them. Don't argue with them, don't try to convince them, just ignore them. Find and surround yourself with people who see what you see and are willing to support you on your journey.

> *"Ignore those that make you fearful and sad, that degrade you back toward disease and death."*
>
> *– Rumi*

CONNECT WITH PEOPLE WHO INSPIRE YOU

Nothing great can be achieved without the help of other people. Reach out to people you admire—people who have achieved the dream that you hope to achieve—and ask them for advice. Asking people for advice and then listening actively is one of the

THE MACRO FOCUS

best ways to connect with them. People love to help; you just need to get into the habit of asking for it.

TAKE A SABBATICAL

Take time off from your work and daily routines. Go to a quiet place and spend some time reflecting and contemplating. Get in touch with your true self. Change your external environment; it will you change your internal environment.

STOP TRYING TO IMPRESS AND START LEARNING

Every human interaction is a potential opportunity to learn, not an opportunity to brag and show off. Learn to ask questions with a child's curiosity and listen actively. People love to tell their stories and share their wisdom, but you have to stop trying to impress them with what you think is great about yourself.

DEVELOP A CREATOR MINDSET

A creator mindset is a mindset of change, growth, and progress. An actor mindset is a mindset of following a script. Creation is an ultimate act of rebellion against the status quo; it's about transcending what exists and creating new ideas and things. Develop a creator mindset by continuously

THE MACRO FOCUS

looking for connections between ideas and concepts to develop new ideas and things that could make life better — for yourself and for the people around you.

SEE YOURSELF AS YOUR FUTURE SELF

You are an emergent phenomenon constantly being shaped by your own words and actions. You create your reality every time you describe yourself. Describe yourself in terms of who you want to be, not who you are today. Start thinking, speaking, dressing, and acting like the person you want to be *before* you become that person.

DON'T CHASE TOO MANY RABBITS

You can achieve anything, but you cannot achieve everything. A wise master once told his pupils that a person who chases two rabbits will catch neither. We live in a very glittery world, and it could all be gold, but you can't go after everything. You must make your choice and say no to the alternatives. In order to achieve greatness, you must focus your energies.

THE MACRO FOCUS

Activities

In the following pages, we will discuss some activities/exercises to help you translate the ideas expressed in preceding pages into practical solutions. You can do these activities alone or in a facilitated workshop setting led by a facilitator.

THE MACRO FOCUS

ACTIVITY: FEELING PROUD

Think of a time when you accomplished or did something that made you feel really proud of yourself.

What was the activity?

What did you do?

How did it make you feel?

THE MACRO FOCUS

ACTIVITY: EMPATHIZING WITH THE OTHER SIDE

Our beliefs have the power to propel us or paralyze us from making progress. Do you have a long held strong belief on some controversial issue? Pick one of those beliefs and pretend, for a moment, that you actually believe in the direct opposite position on that issue. Now write down the reasons why that direct opposite position is justified.

Belief:

Opposite position:

Justifications:
   1.

   2.

   3.

   4.

THE MACRO FOCUS

ACTIVITY: LIFE PURPOSE

Without being humble, complete the following sentence.

The propose of my life is

THE MACRO FOCUS

ACTIVITY: THE WHEEL OF LIFE

Our hectic lifestyles can easily throw our lives off balance. On a scale of one to ten, rate your level of satisfaction in each of the eight dimensions of your life as identified in the following graphic, with one means least satisfied and 10 means highly satisfied. Connect all the dots to see if there is any imbalance, and then reflect on ways to regain balance in your life.

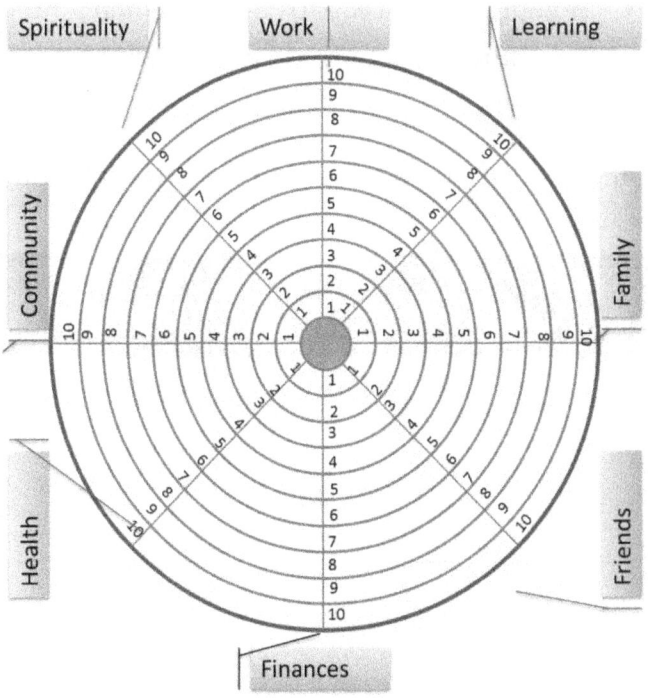

Figure 4: The Wheel of Life

THE MACRO FOCUS

ACTIVITY: FINDING MACRO FOCUS IN KEY FOCUS AREAS OF YOUR LIFE

Without being humble, complete the following table to declare a future vision for the key focus areas of your life.

After your finish writing the vision statement, reflect on the following questions for each vision statement:

- Why do you want to achieve that vision?
- Imagine a few years from now when you have already achieved your vision. How does it feel?
- How would your vision/dream benefit other people?

FOCUS AREA	MACRO FOCUS (VISION/DREAM)
Spiritual	
Family and Friends	

THE MACRO FOCUS

Career	
Lifestyle / Hobby	
Physical Fitness	
Other	

THE MACRO FOCUS

ACTIVITY: DRAW DREAM BOARD

Using words and symbols draw a picture of your Macro Focus/dream/vision. You can use colored markers if you prefer. If the space provided here is not enough, use a separate piece of paper.

When finished, share this picture with your friends and family and explain to them what it means to you.

THE MACRO FOCUS

THE MACRO FOCUS

ACTIVITY: EXPLORING THE MACRO FOCUS

Complete the following form for each one of the Macro Focus areas or dreams.

Macro Focus/Dream Statement:

_____

_____

_____

INTENTION	
Why do I want to achieve this dream?	
What are the key benefits of achieving this dream?	
What could happen if I did not achieve this dream?	
OBSTACLES	
What are the obstacles? What is	

THE MACRO FOCUS

stopping me from taking action?	
RESOURCES	
What resources are already available to me?	
What resources do I need to acquire?	
TARGETS	
Specific targets & timeframes for my dream.	
DREAM TEAM	
Who can help me with my dream? Names of people I will share my dream and progress with.	
ACTIONS	
Three things that I will START doing to achieve this dream	1. 2. 3.
Three things that I will STOP	1.

THE MACRO FOCUS

doing to achieve this dream	2.
	3.

THE MACRO FOCUS

ACTIVITY: DISCOVERING CORE VALUES

Do you know your Core Values? If you are like most people, you may be able to talk about your values, but you probably have never written them down. Well, now is your chance to do it.

The following table lists some of the most common Values that people have. If you need to add more Values to this list, add them in the space provided at the bottom of the table. Read these Values, reflect on them, and mark twelve of these Values that you most care about. Then take another pass, and out of the twelve, choose six Values that are more important than others. These are your Core Values.

After you have identified your Core Values, use the space provided at the bottom of the table to write down a brief paragraph describing what each of the Core Values means to you.

1	2	VALUE NAME	1	2	VALUE NAME
		Adventure			Balance
		Control			Confidence
		Creativity			Discipline
		Education			Faith
		Family			Financial Security

THE MACRO FOCUS

1	2	VALUE NAME	1	2	VALUE NAME
		Friends			Freedom
		Fulfillment			Forgiveness
		Fun			Growth
		Happiness			Health
		Hope			Honesty
		Humor			Independence
		Integrity			Kindness
		Knowledge			Marriage
		Peace of mind			Power
		Progress			Reason
		Security			Self-reliance
		Service			Spirituality
		Strength			Success
		Truth			Wisdom

Write a brief paragraph describing what each of the selected Core Values means to you.

1. Core Value One:

THE MACRO FOCUS

2. Core Value Two:

3. Core Value Three:

4. Core Value Four:

5. Core Value Five:

6. Core Value Six:

CHAPTER FOUR

The Micro Focus

BUILDING HABITS FOR OPTIMAL RESULTS

THE MICRO FOCUS

"Tomorrow belongs to those who prepare for it today."

– Malcolm X

The Micro Focus is the roadmap to your destination. It's what needs to be done, every day, in order to achieve your Macro Focus. Having a dream is great, but nothing happens until you take action and perform activities that help you move toward your dream. Micro Focus is where rubber meets the road. It's where you identify and commit to doing what needs to be done in order to achieve your dreams. Finding your Macro Focus is a great start; right *intention* must be in place, but right results can only be produced by the right *action*.

THE MICRO FOCUS

Being born again is not just once in a lifetime activity; you are born again every morning. Every day is your chance to recreate yourself. Yesterday is gone; it's only a memory. What is real is today. Today gives you another opportunity to take

> *"Ignore those that make you fearful and sad, that degrade you back towards disease and death."*
>
> *— Rumi*

the right actions. You can choose to simply react to whatever the world throws at you, or you can choose to design your day the way you intend it to be. Micro Focus is the art of designing your day based on who you want to be and what you want to achieve. When you commit to a focused life, your actions are driven by your intention. In other words, your Macro Focus drives your Micro Focus.

The secret to finding your Micro Focus is not in finding more things to do; it's in finding the non-essential and eliminating it. This creates space and time needed for what is essential. When these essential things are done on regular basis, they evolve into habits.

What is a habit?

THE MICRO FOCUS

A habit is a routine behavior or a settled pattern that happens subconsciously or automatically. It's the thing that you do without thinking. We can see a habit in action when we look at both sides of the street before crossing it.

> *"Sayings remain meaningless until they are embodied in habits."*
>
> – Khalil Gibran

A habit is a learned behavior. New habits are formed when certain behaviors are repeated on a regular basis. Getting rid of bad habits and forming new habits is not an easy task, as someone who is trying to quit smoking can certainly tell you, but it's very important, as habits hold the key to sustainable behavior transformation. Good habits can put the good behavior on autopilot, making change lasting and fun.

Every day provides you with an opportunity to start fresh and recreate yourself. All you have to do is to make yourself better than your yesterday self. Your yesterday-self is the only person you need to compare yourself with. Comparing yourself with anyone else is futile and will only bring frustration

THE MICRO FOCUS

and sadness, as there will always be someone who is better than you in something.

Before you decide to spend any of your time and energy on anything, make sure it is both meaningful (it helps you move toward your dream) and it's controllable (you can actually do something about it). As for the rest of the stuff, just ignore it; life is too short to waste time on things that you can't control or are not meaningful.

Let's look at the key benefits of living a life with Micro Focus:

- You learn that what produces big results is not really the intelligence; it's the focus and continuous effort in pursuing things that help you more toward your desired future state.

- You learn from your mistakes. You may not hit the target the first time but a clear target and continuous effort will lead to the refinement of your approach over time.

- Over time your commitment and motivation increases. Your willpower is limited; it's the continuous progress that provides sustained

THE MICRO FOCUS

motivation and keeps you going.

- As you eliminate things that are not adding value, you gain control over you time and day.

- You move from doing what seems easy to doing what is right. In the beginning, what is right may not be easy, but if you persist, what is right ultimately becomes easy and fun.

- When you set and complete your tasks for the day, you will feel a sense of accomplishment, progress, and gratitude.

THE MICRO FOCUS

The Obstacles

NOT DOING THE PROPER RESEARCH

Having a Macro Focus or a clearly identified vision/dream is one thing. Knowing what needs to be done to achieve that vision is something totally different. Just following someone else who seems to be heading the same way does not always work either. Each person and each situation is different. Many people do things that seem right but don't always produce the desired results.

LACK OF CLARITY

It's been said that if you don't know where you are going, it does not matter which road you take. If there is a lack of clarity about the target, it would not be easy to figure out what is important and what isn't.

FEAR OF MISSING OUT

Fear of missing out is one of the key reasons people struggle with their Micro Focus. They try to be everywhere and do everything because they don't want to miss out on anything. You see some people

THE MICRO FOCUS

who make sure they attend every meeting whether they add any value or not. They want to be at every party even when there are more important things to take care of.

> *"The art of knowing is knowing what to ignore."*
>
> *– Rumi*

PROCRASTINATION

We all procrastinate to a certain degree, but some people develop the habit of engaging in more pleasurable activities and putting off important tasks. They lack the self-control and discipline to tackle what they know they must do.

CONSTANT DISTRACTION

Sometimes people struggle to find their Micro Focus because they work in an environment that attracts distractions. Instead of focusing on what they need to do they get used to getting their energy from what distracts them from what is important.

NOT UNDERSTANDING THE 'OPPORTUNITY COST'

There are activities that help you move toward your vision/dream, and then there are activities that take you away from it. These two are relatively easy to

THE MICRO FOCUS

figure out. The real challenge is the vast middle where an activity is somewhat helpful and does add some value. The challenge some people face is their inability to understand the concept of opportunity cost — the loss of potential gain that could have come from another activity. Time is a limited resource; it is used optimally only when a chosen activity is not only valuable but also *more* valuable than all other options.

Suggestions for Finding Micro Focus

START YOUR DAY RIGHT

Start your day with a clear intention, gratitude, and motivation. When you start your day with a plan and motivation to do things that will help you move toward your dream, you declare an intention to be in charge of your own life.

Life is going to throw things at you that you might have to respond to, but start your day off by telling yourself and the universe about what matters to you.

The best way to accomplish this is to create a personal ritual.

What is a personal ritual?

A personal ritual is a set of actions performed regularly in a precise manner on your own. A personal ritual helps you prime for the day ahead. Whether your personal priming ritual is rooted in a faith tradition, or something that you create through trial and error, it is wonderful tool to get ready for

THE MICRO FOCUS

the day.

Here is how famous motivational speaker Tony Robbins puts it;

> "*I made a deal with myself: If you don't have 10 minutes for yourself, you don't have a life.*"

There countless ways you can create your own personal morning ritual.

Here are some ideas

- Praying: Seek help and strength for the opportunities and challenges that lies ahead.
- Sitting silently: Sit silently in a comfortable position doing nothing. Just notice all the sensations in your body and the sounds smells of what surrounds you.
- Breathing: Sit in comfortable position and take a set number of deep breaths.
- Being grateful: Count three things in your life that you are grateful for.
- Exercising: This could be any number of things: yoga, stretching, pushups, running,

THE MICRO FOCUS

etc.

You can pick anything form the list above or create new activities, the key is to perform same set of activities in the same manner every day. Just like

> *"If a man does not know to what port he is steering; no wind is favorable to him."*
>
> – Seneca

a good painter who uses a primer before he applies the actual paint, a focused person needs a positive morning ritual to get ready for the day.

USE THE 80/20 RULE

The 80/20 rule, also known as the Pareto principle, is a great model to understand what really matters and where we should invest our time and energy. It was originally introduced by Italian economist Vilfredo Pareto who observed that almost 80% of the effects come from 20% of the causes. The 80/20 rule has been extended and extrapolated to explain many other things. According to this principle, since 20 percent of things we do account for 80 percent of value, we can achieve significantly more with much less effort by focusing our efforts on the 20 percent that truly matters.

THE MICRO FOCUS

Become familiar with this rule. Figure out which 20 percent of your activities are producing 80 percent of the results in your life. Focus on those 20 percent of the activities, and your results will grow exponentially.

CREATE A "TODAY LIST"

Create a list of activates that must be done today. This is a list focused on activities that you must perform today in order to achieve your dream. A Today-List encourages habit-building; a To-Do-List just creates stress by documenting everything that is not done yet. Try to keep your list limited to three to five items. Other things will create their own space. If you have only a few items on your list, you are more likely to actually do them and do them in a focused way. Focus on the big rocks; the pebbles will find their spot.

Where possible put these activities on your schedule, so you have a block of time set aside for each one of these activities.

THE MICRO FOCUS

CREATE A "TO-BE LIST"

Your Today-List is a list of *what* you want to do, but life is not just about doing things. It's really a journey toward being what we ought to be as human beings. Use your *To-Be-List* as a reminder to always be a kinder, gentler, and caring person as you go through your day. Here are some of the things that you can put on your To-Be-List:

> "Think before you speak- "Before you speak, let your words pass through three gates. At the first gate, ask yourself, 'Is it true?' At the second gate ask, 'Is it necessary?' At the third gate ask, 'Is it kind?'"
>
> – A Sufi Quote

- Be kind.
- Be organized.
- Be fun to be around.
- Be approachable.
- Be positive.
- Be confident.
- Be respectful.
- Be a good listener.

THE MICRO FOCUS

- Be open to learning.
- Be creative.
- Be helpful.

Try limiting your *To-Be List* to only one item every day. This *list* will serve as a reminder of the kind of person you want to be as you pursue your dreams.

> *"Most of what we say and do is not essential. If you can eliminate it, you'll have more time, and more tranquility. Ask yourself at every moment, 'Is this necessary?'"*
>
> – Marcus Aurelius, Meditations

KEEP IT SHORT AND SIMPLE (KISS)

We are conditioned to do things a certain way, but no matter how great you think your way of doing things is, there is always a simpler way to achieve similar or better outcomes. Many of us are busy because we are trying to make things bigger and more complex. Try to keep it simple.

Time and energy are limited resources; you must be very efficient in using them. Develop a mindset of finding the simplest way to perform every task.

USE THE CREATOR LANGUAGE

Instead of using expressions like "I need to" or "I

THE MICRO FOCUS

have to", use creator language such as "I choose to", "I decide to", and "I will" when deciding to do things. Creator words give you a sense of control and choice; non-creator words leave you at the mercy of circumstances.

CREATE A MONITORING SYSTEM

No one ever hits the target with their eyes closed. You must create a system to keep an eye on key measures of success and adjust your course if you are not making progress. For example, if you are trying to achieve optimal health, here are some of the number easy to monitor metrics:

1. Resting Heart Rate
2. Sleep
3. Daily Steps
4. Weight
5. Body Fat Percentage
6. Daily Calorie Intake
7. Cholesterol
8. Blood Sugar Level

Of course there are many more metrics you might

THE MICRO FOCUS

have to track based on your personal situation, but key point here is to not to just guess your progress toward you goal, let numbers tell the story. Build a system to monitor your progress. And if numbers don't show a positive trend, it's time to try something else.

AVOID DECISION FATIGUE

Decision making consumes a lot of mental resources. There are only a certain number of decisions you can make in a day without suffering from decision fatigue. To reduce this number of decisions, make them quickly and in batches, automate things, and stick to routines when it comes to non-essentials.

Talking about the importance of de-cluttering habits, and the need for reducing the number of daily decisions that he has to make, President Barak Obama said in a recent interview that he only wears blue or gray suits. "You need to focus your decision-making energy. You need to routinize yourself," he told *Vanity Fair*.

GO HIGH-TECH

Using a paper-based Today-List can give you a quick start, but these days there are so many great

THE MICRO FOCUS

technology-based options available that make monitoring and tracking of tasks a much richer experience.

> *"Trade your expectation for appreciation and the world changes instantly."*
>
> *— Tony Robbins*

If you own a smartphone, here are some of the apps that you might want to try:

1. Wunderlist
2. HabitRPG
3. Balanced
4. Any.do
5. Google Keep
6. Microsoft To-Do

BE GRATEFUL

Life is not about endless struggle to find answers to complex questions. Life is a mystery. Don't try to solve it; just learn to cherish it. Enjoy the gullibility of absolutists, the confusion of doubters, and be grateful that you have the wisdom to observe it without getting sucked into it.

THE MICRO FOCUS

Create a ritual to count your blessings. Every morning, before your start your day, sit down in a quiet place, close your eyes for few seconds, take three long breaths, and then count three of your blessing.

BE PLAYFUL

If you are not enjoying what you are doing, ultimately you are going to give it up. Humor and playfulness are sometime viewed as mundane activities that ordinary people engage in. Nothing can be further from the truth. Playfulness is the path that leads to true wisdom. Humor is the ability to appreciate and express what makes people laugh. Only very wise people are capable of finding humor in what they do and what happens in the world around them.

Focused people go through their day with positivity, cheer, and laughter; they are relaxed and nonjudgmental; they are curious but content; they are appreciative of their colleagues, friends, and family. They know how to play and laugh. Their laughter comes from calm place deep inside their hearts. If laughter is not coming from a calm, and tranquil place, it is a laughter that is at the expense

THE MICRO FOCUS

of someone else. This type of laughter is cruel and hurtful.

If you approach the world from the vantage point of curiosity, love and gratitude, every activity is a celebration; every relationship is awesome; every day is fantastic; every walk is memorable; and every joke is funny. There is nothing to worry about. Let go of the need to be right all the time. Celebrate the freedom to experiment, make mistakes, the freedom to be non-serious, the freedom to contradict yourself, the freedom to be wrong, the freedom to laugh, and the freedom to learn from your mistakes and change course.

THE MICRO FOCUS

Activities

ACTIVITY: SWOT ANALYSIS

Strengths, Weakness, Opportunities, and Threats (SWOT) Analysis is a powerful strategic planning tool that can be used for self-analysis and accurate appraisal of the current situation.

This is not an exercise in modesty; be honest with your answers, as this information helps establish the baseline against which you can measure your progress.

Strengths

- What do you do well?
- What unique skills do you have that can help you with your dream/vision?
- What do you enjoy doing?

Weaknesses

- What can you do better?
- What do people see as your weakness?
- What do you not like doing?

THE MICRO FOCUS

Opportunities

- What opportunities are available to you currently?
- Are there any training/coaching opportunities available in your office or school?
- Are there any strengths that you can turn into opportunities?

Threats

- Is there anything that can derail you from your journey?
- Are there any bad habits that have stopped you from making progress in the past?
- Are there any changing priorities/future responsibilities that could take your focus away from your journey?
-

STRENGTHS
•
•
•

THE MICRO FOCUS

-

WEAKNESSES

-
-
-
-

OPPORTUNITIES

-
-
-
-

THREATS

-
-
-
-

THE MICRO FOCUS

ACTIVITY: FINDING MICRO FOCUS & BUILDING NEW HABITS

List the activities you will need to perform on a daily or regular basis in order to achieve the vision in key focus areas of your life as identified in the previous activities in the Macro Focus chapter.

Focus Area: Spirituality

Vision/Dream:

_____

_____

Actions:

1.
2.
3.

Focus Area: Work

Vision/Dream:

_____

_____

Actions:

1.

THE MICRO FOCUS

2.

3.

Focus Area: Learning

Vision/Dream:

_____

_____

Actions:

1.

2.

3.

Focus Area: Family

Vision/Dream:

_____

_____

Actions:

1.

2.

3.

Focus Area: Friends

THE MICRO FOCUS

Vision/Dream:
_____
_____

Actions:

    7.

    8.

    9.

Focus Area: Finances

Vision/Dream:
_____
_____

Actions:

    1.

    2.

    3.

Focus Area: Health

Vision/Dream:
_____
_____

THE MICRO FOCUS

Actions:

1.
2.
3.

Focus Area: Community

Vision/Dream:

_____

_____

Actions:

1.
2.
3.

THE MICRO FOCUS

ACTIVITY: WHERE DOES MY TIME GO

Nature is very fair; we all get 24 hours in a day and 168 hours in a week. What makes the difference is what we do with that time. No one is really busy; some people just focus on the wrong things. Use the following tool to understand how you spend your time. Then reflect on the following questions to identify and eliminate your time wasters.

- Am I spending enough time on things that truly matter?
- What can I do to make things better?

THE MICRO FOCUS

ACTIVITY	DAILY TIME	WEEKLY TIME
Sleep		
Grooming/Body-care		
Commute		
Housekeeping activities at work		
Work on projects		
Meetings		
Cooking		
Eating		
Shopping		
Family/child care		
Fun & Leisure		
Other		
Other		
Other		
TOTAL		

CHAPTER FIVE

The Nano Focus

BEING IN THE PRESENT MOMENT

THE NANO FOCUS

"How foolish is man! He ruins the present while worrying about the future, but weeps in the future by recalling his past."

– Ali Ibn Abi Talib

There is an old tale about a king who wanted to find answers to the questions that he believed were the most important questions a man could ask. He announced that anyone who would answer his questions would be rewarded generously. The questions were:

THE NANO FOCUS

1. What is the most important time?
2. Who is the most important person?
3. What is the most important task?

Many wise people came forward and tried to answer these questions but the king was not satisfied. Finally, he learned about a wise old man who lived alone in a distant valley. The king dressed as an ordinary man and went to see him. After meeting the wise man, the king asked his questions. The wise man looked into the king's eyes and said that this was really simple:

1. The most important time is the present time.
2. The most important person is the person you are with.
3. The most important task is the task that you are working on.

What a profound answer! And in that answer, lies the essence of the idea of Nano Focus. Simply put, the Nano Focus is about being in the present moment and doing the task at hand with utmost focus, attention, and concentration.

Life happens in the present moment — neither in the

THE NANO FOCUS

past nor in the future, but in the now, in the present moment. The past is gone and the future is just an idea or a hope at best. You never really see it except in the form of present. If you are not living in the present moment, you are not living. You are just stuck in the dark abyss of your mind. The quality of your life is dependent on your ability to be in the present moment with a positive psychological state. The quality of your experience depends on the level of focus you bring to the activity you are engaged in.

> *"Concentrate all your thoughts upon the work at hand. The sun's rays do not burn until brought to a focus."*
>
> *– Alexander Graham Bell*

Nano Focus is the art of being *here* and *now* and doing meaningful activities with complete attention. It's about being mindful of the desired future but not fearing it. It's about being mindful of the lessons of the past but not reliving it.

The Nano Focus is obviously not a new concept; it's been studied and taught for thousands of years in various spiritual and wisdom traditions. If we go back in history, we find that Buddha taught the same

THE NANO FOCUS

concept to the people in Northern India 2,500 years ago. It has been said that, at one time, a visitor asked Buddha what he and his followers did when they got together. Buddha looked at him with a gentle smile and said, "When we are together, we sit, we eat, and we walk." The visitor was completely puzzled by Buddha's answer. He did not expect such a simplistic-sounding answer from a wise man like Buddha. He implored Buddha further and asked, "How is that special? Everyone does that." Sensing his puzzlement, Buddha explained, "When we sit, we know that we are sitting; when we eat, we know we are eating; and when we walk, we know that we are walking."

What was Buddha trying to teach that person? He was teaching a simple lesson in Nano Focus: It's not just what you do; it's also how you do it, what mindfulness you bring to what you do, what focus you bring to what you do. The difference between extraordinary and ordinary is the focus. An ordinary activity becomes extraordinary if we bring the right awareness to it. And an extraordinary activity becomes ordinary if we don't do it with focus and mindfulness.

THE NANO FOCUS

The famous Urdu poet Faiz once said:

> *What is everlasting is the grace with which you walk toward your execution chamber.*
>
> *Life has to end anyway; it really is no big deal.*

How does Nano Focus make a difference? Well, let's talk about a simple activity of taking a walk in the park. Most people go to the park for a walk, and the only thing they get out of it is a little bit of physical activity. Their body is in the park, but their mind is not there. They are still thinking about all sorts of stuff: unpaid bills, bad economy, law-and-order situations, work, etc. Their mind is either regretting the past or is fearful of the future; it's not enjoying the beautiful present, which is right in front of them. They hardly notice anything in the park — the flowers, the birds, the breeze, the sunset — everything goes unnoticed.

A walk with focus and presence is a walk that rejuvenates and refreshes. It connects you with nature. When you walk with focus, your mind is not wandering around. It's right there with you in the

THE NANO FOCUS

park. When you walk with Nano Focus, you feel the breeze on your face. You let the whiff of nature overtake you. You touch the trees and leaves and feel their freshness. You listen to the sounds of birds and insects. You savor the sights of the beautiful sunset. You use all of your senses to be part of the present moment. Your focus is in what you are doing at that very moment. You become one with the park. You become the park.

> *"Ardently do today what must be done. Who knows? Tomorrow, death comes."*
>
> *– Buddha*

In the same way, you can eat food the ordinary way, with a mind full of endless chatter and useless thoughts, or you can eat it with mindfulness and focus. When you eat your food with focus, you start off by being thankful for the food. You look into the eyes and connect with the people at the table. You touch your food to feel its texture; you smell its aroma and relish its taste. You praise the cook for preparing the delicious food. An ordinary dinner eaten with focus becomes an extraordinary dinner.

Here is how Hafiz, the famous Sufi poet, describes

THE NANO FOCUS

listening with focus:

> *How do I listen to others?*
>
> *As if everyone was my master,*
>
> *Speaking to me his cherished last words.*

Everything in life can be a miracle for you, and you can choose to live it with presence, with focus. Every experience can become optimal if the right mindset is applied to it.

As Rumi once reminded the world:

> *This We Have Now*
>
> *This we have now is not imagination.*
>
> *This is not grief or joy.*
>
> *Not a judging state, or an elation, or sadness.*
>
> *Those come and go.*
>
> *This is the presence that doesn't.*

Most of us have tried or at least heard of benefits of yoga, meditation, Zen, and other contemplative practices. While there is no doubt that these practices

THE NANO FOCUS

are generally good and very helpful tools against stress and distraction, practicing them is not a panacea for every known human ailment. All of these contemplative practices are about *clearing the mind,* which is, of course, a

> *"Zen is not some kind of excitement, but concentration on our usual everyday routine."*
>
> *— Shunryu Suzuki*

critical first step in an increasingly distracting and befuddling world. It's like a farmer clearing the unwanted weeds from the soil before he can sow seeds for the crop he wants. A person who believes that somehow practicing these contemplative methods is an end in itself is like a farmer who clears the soil of weeds but never plants the seeds — a rather mindless activity.

Nano Focus is mindfulness with a purpose. It's not just about doing things; it's about doing the *right* things with optimal focus and attention.

Here is a summary of some of the key benefits of finding and living a life of Nano Focus:

- You start noticing things and become more thankful for what you already have.

THE NANO FOCUS

- Once your mind is quiet and free from the regrets of the past and the fears of the future, your soul will start speaking. You will begin to build a deeper relationship with the real you.

> *"We are what we repeatedly do. Excellence, then, is not an act but a habit."*
>
> *— Aristotle*

- You realize that the present moment is all you have; everything else is either a memory or a hope. So, you slow down and start enjoying life as it happens.

- You learn to get in touch with your emotions and evolve to a higher degree of self-awareness and emotional intelligence.

- You realize that multitasking is just an illusion—just a fancy word for distraction. What really happens is that you switch from one task to another, without paying full attention to either one of them. But when you start single-tasking and bring full attention to the task at hand, the quality of your work improves tremendously and you

THE NANO FOCUS

get a lot more done.

Let's now look at some of the most common obstacles people face in their journey to finding their Nano Focus.

The Obstacles

THE ENVIRONMENT

Nano Focus requires preparation. The physical environment of the space where activity is being performed has a huge impact on the quality of focus. A noisy and cluttered room with too many sparkly, shiny objects is certainly not very conducive to focused work.

POOR NUTRITION

Lack of proper nutrition can be a big obstacle in finding the Nano Focus. Hunger limits the ability to concentrate.

OVER COMMITMENT

Oftentimes, over commitment is a major source of distraction. When people have too many things they are committed to, they are not likely to bring their full concentration to the task at hand.

HABIT OF RESPONDING TO EVERYTHING

Not every email, text message, or phone call deserves a response. Some people get addicted to

THE NANO FOCUS

constant stimulation that they get by attending and responding to a constant barrage of communication, which ultimately takes their focus away from the activity they should be focused on.

> *"Be empty of worrying.*
>
> *Think of who created thought!*
>
> *Why do you stay in prison?*
>
> *When the door is so wide open?"*
>
> *– Rumi*

TOO MUCH WORRYING

Worrying too much about things that cannot be controlled is a sure way to sabotage the quality of what is *here* and *now*. Worrying too much does not solve any problems; it only creates new ones by jeopardizing the quality of the work at hand.

MENTAL RESTLESSNESS

Some people have a monkey mind — a restless mind that is constantly hopping from one thought to another. How can you experience sights, sounds and smells of the present moment if your mind is busy in thought hopping?

THE NANO FOCUS

PHYSICAL RESTLESSNESS

It's hard to concentrate if the body is tired and fatigued. Some people struggle with their Nano Focus because they leave important tasks for the end of the day when their body is tired and energy levels are low.

THE NANO FOCUS

Suggestions for Finding the Nano Focus

HAVE A CLEAR INTENT TO FOCUS

Remind yourself why it's important for you to pay full attention to the task at hand. Say a prayer or the phrase that works for you. You can use any of the following phrases or create your own if you prefer.

- I intend to bring my full attention to this task.
- I intend to be here now.
- I'm here.

CREATE AN OPTIMAL WORKING ENVIRONMENT

Your physical environment has an enormous impact on your ability to focus. Here are some specific actions you can take to create an optimal environment;

- Play instrumental music or nature sounds as

THE NANO FOCUS

> white noise to conceal other distracting sounds.

- Avoid putting too many unnecessary posters/pictures on the walls.

> *"When walking, walk. When eating, eat."*
>
> *– Zen Proverb*

- Certain smells/fragrances can boost concentration. Find out what works for you and use it to enhance your environment.
- Keep everything tidy and clean.
- Make sure you sit in a comfortable chair.

TAKE CARE OF YOUR NUTRITIONAL NEEDS

Eat a healthy breakfast and make sure you are properly nourished. Healthy snacks, coffee, and water could help boost your concentration.

DON'T DWELL ON THE PAST

Staying stuck in the past lowers the quality of the present moment for many people. Non-stop reminiscence of the past rarely adds any value to the present or the future. Do remember the positive experiences and the lessons from the past, but forget

THE NANO FOCUS

the rest. As a society, we are too focused on re-living and sometimes repairing the past. If you really want to optimize your life, shift your focus to creating the future instead.

> *"A Sufi was asked what forgiveness is. He said, it is the fragrance that flowers give when they are crushed."*
>
> — Anonymous

PERFORM A RITUAL BEFORE YOU START AN ACTIVITY

Create a ritual that works for you before you begin the new activity or task. Your intention is your internal reminder to focus whereas your ritual is the external reminder — a physical activity — that it's time to focus on the new activity. What kind of internal or external reminder you use is not as important as the fact that you need to remind yourself that it's time to pay your full attention to what's coming up next.

Here are some ideas for the ritual:

- Take three deep breaths.
- Rub your palms together.
- Close your eyes for few seconds.

THE NANO FOCUS

- Rub your forehead for few seconds.

DON'T LEAVE TASKS UNFINISHED

Unfinished tasks take up space in your mind and can create a worry loop. A Russian psychologist, Zeigarnik, who studied waiters, found out that a waiter was more likely to recall incomplete orders than served ones (Zeigarnik, 1927). In psychology, this is known as the Zeigarnik effect. A follow-up study confirmed that people are 90 percent more likely to remember unfinished tasks than completed ones. So, finish what you start before moving on to the next task.

FORGIVE, LEARN, FORGET, AND MOVE ON

Many people struggle with Micro Focus because they are stuck in the wrongs of the past. They cannot get over the wrong done to them no matter how much time has passed or they cannot forgive themselves if they wronged someone else. Here is the news: the past is over. And you need to move on too. Here is a simple process to accomplish it.

If you did something wrong to someone, follow the acronym S.L.F.:

- S - Seek forgiveness and forgive yourself.

THE NANO FOCUS

- L - Learn the lesson.
- F - Forget it and move on.

If someone else did something wrong to you, the acronym you want to remember is F.L.F.:

- F - Forgive them.
- L - Learn the lesson.
- F - Forget it and move on.

Learn the art of accepting an apology without ever receiving it. Why? Because it's good for you! You need to forgive people not necessarily because they deserve forgiveness, but because you deserve peace of mind.

X-OUT THE WORD FEAR

Fear of the future is another major source of distraction. Do yourself a favor and remove the word *fear* from your vocabulary, and replace it with the word *aware*. Be aware of and be prepared for the potential risks but never be afraid of anything.

Irrational fear of the future is a uniquely human affliction and a major factor behind people inability to focus. Most fears are literally a figment of human

THE NANO FOCUS

imagination. They need not exist. Planning is good; nothing wrong with planning, but don't ruin your present with irrational fears of the future. What is the worst that could happen—you won't reach your goal? But if you've enjoyed the process and learned the lesson, have you really failed? Most of the things that people waste their lives fearing never really materialize. So don't waste the precious little time that you have on this earth fearing the future; just be aware of the risks, and focus on the present.

PLAY GAMES

Almost all sports and games help strengthen mental muscles for better focus and concentration. But certain games such as chess are particularly helpful in training the brain for Nano Focus. Find out what works for you and make time to do it on a regular basis.

START REGULAR EXERCISE

Exercise, especially one that involves serious strength training, is a great way to clear your mind of the regrets of the past and the fears of the future. It's hard to not be in the present moment when you are pushing heavy weights off your chest. Exercise not only trains your body, it also trains your mind to

THE NANO FOCUS

be in the present.

FIX THE SOURCE OF YOUR DISTRACTION

Sometimes there is that one unresolved issue that keeps bothering you and taking your focus away from the task at hand. Stop everything and resolve that issue first. Procrastinating on something that cannot wait will be sure way to stay distracted.

TAKE BREAKS

Your energy is limited; spend it wisely. Take occasional breaks. Go out for a brief walk in nature, stretch, close your eyes and take a deep breath, chat with a friend, do what feels natural to you. Taking breaks helps you reenergize and start off the task with better focus and concentration.

Taking a break is especially important when you find yourself overwhelmed by a situation. In that case, your best option is to go SOBER. Here is what it means:

S - Stop.

O - Observe yourself and the situation.

B - Breath in and out deeply for at least three times.

THE NANO FOCUS

E - Examine your emotions and ensure you are in charge of your emotions, not the other way around.

R - Resume the task again.

PRACTICE ACTIVE LISTENING

Active listening means asking intelligent questions, listening attentively, and making sure the conversation stays focused on achieving predefined outcomes.

Active listening is not just pretending to be listening and waiting for your turn to speak, but *actually* listening with your full attention and focus, with the intent to understand. Don't judge, don't interrupt, don't think—just listen; because when you are actively listening, you are not thinking. Think about it.

THE NANO FOCUS

Activities

ACTIVITY: COUNTING FORWARD AND BACKWARD

Find a quiet place to sit comfortably. Close your eyes and count to 100. After you reach one hundred, count backward from 100 to 1. Do this without thinking about anything else. Keep your full focus on counting the numbers. You can close your eyes if you prefer.

After you finish the activity, answer the following questions;

- Did you find the activity easy or difficult?
- Why do you think the activity was easy or difficult for you?
- Can you count the number of times you found yourself thinking about other things?
- How do you feel now?

THE NANO FOCUS

ACTIVITY: DEEP BREATHING

Deep breathing is one of the simplest ways to clear your mind of unwanted mental chatter and to bring your focus back to the present moment. Deep breathing provides the additional flow of oxygen your body needs to rejuvenate and enjoy the benefits of aerobic exercise.

Follow these steps:

- Sit in a comfortable and balanced position.
- Close your eyes.
- Take a long, deep breath—long and deep enough to fill your chest with air without making you uncomfortable.
- Pause and feel how it affects your body.
- Breathe out and observe how your body changes.
- Take a few more breaths and keep your focus on the air going in as you inhale and going out as you exhale. Observe how it affects your body.
- If unwanted thoughts pop up into your head, don't fight them—just push them away

THE NANO FOCUS

gently and bring the focus back to breathing.

- Practice this for five to ten minutes and write down how you feel afterward:

_____

_____

_____

_____

THE NANO FOCUS

ACTIVITY: FULL CONCENTRATION

Pick an activity, in the house or at work, and commit to doing it with 100% concentration and focus. During that activity you should not be thinking about anything else in the world; there should be no past regrets or future worries.

When finished, reflect on the following questions:

- How successful were you?
- Did it change the quality of your work?
- What kind of thoughts came to your mind?
- What can you do differently to improve you focus in the future?

CHAPTER SIX

Putting It All Together

LEARNING THE TOOLS OF THE TRQDE

PUTTING IT ALL TOGETHER

"Happiness cannot be travelled to, owned, earned, or worn. It is the spiritual experience of living every minute with love, grace, and gratitude."

– Denis Waitley

What is the biggest problem with motivation? Well, I think we all know the answer to that...*it does not last.* You read a book, attend a seminar or talk to someone who inspires you, and you are ready to change things once and for all. But for some reason, after a

PUTTING IT ALL TOGETHER

few days or weeks, motivation wears off and you find yourself in the same rut again. As a matter of fact, the data in this regard is quite startling. As

> *"What we speak becomes the house we live in."*
>
> *— Hāfez*

mentioned before, according to a study conducted by the University of Scranton and published in the *Journal of Clinical Psychology,* only 8% of Americans who make New Year resolutions are likely to succeed. That's an abysmal success rate by any standard.

While setting goals and New Year resolutions itself is not the problem, what is a problem is the inability to follow up with any consistent and systematic way. The challenge most people face is not the lack of goals or desires; it's the lack of a *system* to follow through and actualize those goals and desires.

So far we have covered a lot of information in this book. This chapter is aimed at bringing it all together into a simple framework and tool that anyone can use. It's called *The DREAM System. The DREAM System is a* tool to visualize, plan and actualize dreams. Just like an organization's strategic plan,

PUTTING IT ALL TOGETHER

which sets out the vision, missions, and objectives for the organization, this tool helps you build your personal strategic plan. You can use this plan on your own, using the information provided here, or you could work with a trained coach to help you through the process.

The DREAM System lays out a four-step process for building your personal plan. It provides a framework to visualize and logically connect key elements of Focusology.

It's a tool for sustainable behavioral change that is baked in science with an elegant user interface.

Let's look at the visual:

PUTTING IT ALL TOGETHER

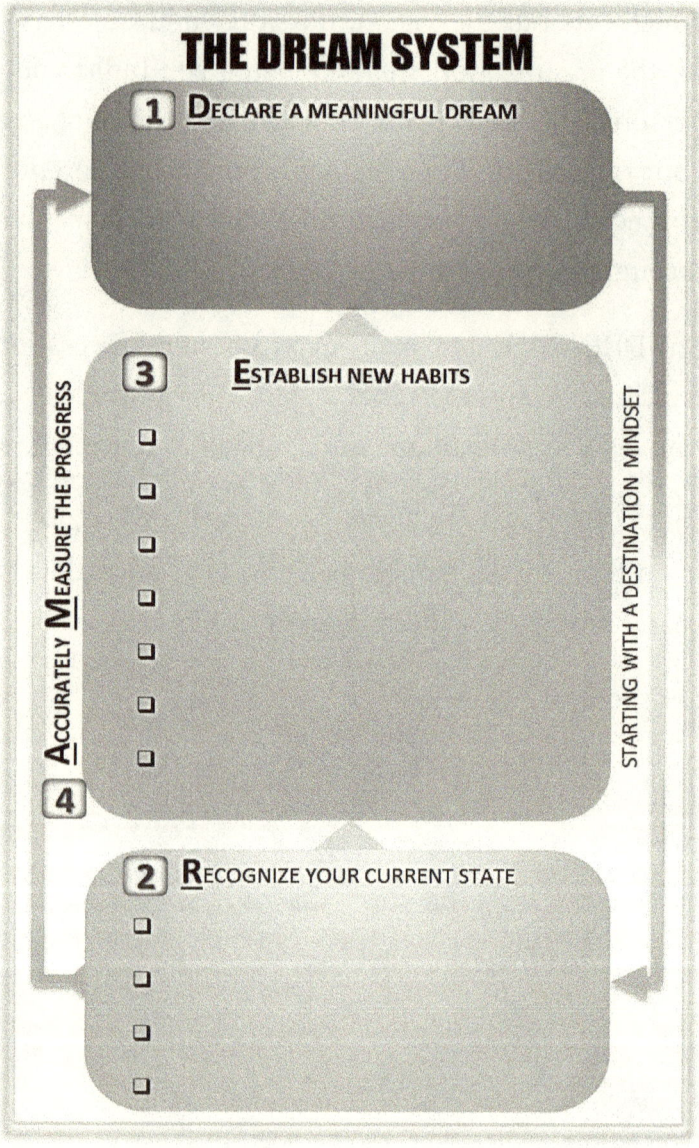

Figure 5: The DREAM System

PUTTING IT ALL TOGETHER

The first step, as we have discussed, in your journey to a better *you* starts with finding a Macro Focus. The best way to climb a mountain is to start from the top. In other words, begin with the end in mind, as Dr Stephen Covey has reminded us in his best-selling book *The Seven Habits of Highly Effective People*. Write your Macro Focus/dream/vision statement using action verbs: achieve, be, write, develop, support, empower, help, etc. It could look something like…

> *"Mastering others is strength. Mastering yourself is true power."*
>
> – Lao Tzu

"Become a great writer."

Or it could be any vision or dream you want to achieve in any area of your life.

"Achieve optimal health."

Either way, make sure what you write is positive, holistic, and inspirational, because it's the power of your dream that is going to pull you along when the going gets tough.

PUTTING IT ALL TOGETHER

The second step is to fully recognize and understand your current state. As you undertake the journey of change, it's important to know who you are, where you stand, what resources you have, what your strengths and weakness are. There is more than one way to achieve this objective.

> "Nothing is more harmful to the service, than the neglect of discipline; for that discipline, more than numbers, gives one army superiority over another."
>
> – George Washington

No one knows you better than yourself, so self-reflection is your primary tool here. Seeking 360-degree feedback, also known as multi-rater feedback, from people who know you is also a great way to start. You can also consider taking personality/psychometric assessments. Personality assessment can help reveal an individual's psychological makeup and suggest ways to address areas of concern.

After you have completed Step Two, it's time to figure out what actions need to be taken to achieve your vision. This is your Micro Focus. This is where

PUTTING IT ALL TOGETHER

you list actions, activities, and initiatives that you will undertake on a regular basis to achieve your dream.

Knowledge is good, but knowledge does not really change anything. The secret to any sustainable behavior change lies in the adoption of new routines and habits.

It's always better to think big but start small. Your first task here is to reprogram your brain and change your habitual patterns of thinking and behaving. So, start small—really small. For example: If you want to do 100 pushups, start with doing one push-up every day, at a fixed time. This will help you establish the new habit without scaring you about what could be perceived as an enormous task ahead.

One of the ways to start your journey is to model the behavior of those who already are what you want to be. But make sure you only use it as a starting point; their journey was their journey and your journey is your journey. Learning from others is good, slavish adherence to their ways of doing is not. Learn the rules first, but never be afraid of challenging them. Always respect those who are what you want to be but be careful about revering them…reverence can

PUTTING IT ALL TOGETHER

stifle your creativity and growth.

Stay focused on what is meaningful and what you can control. Ignore what does not meet these two conditions.

The last step in the system deals with accurately measuring the progress. What gets measured gets done, as they say. Being able to accurately monitor

> *"You can be anything you want to be, if only you believe with sufficient conviction and act in accordance with your faith; for whatever the mind can conceive and believe, the mind can achieve."*
>
> *— Napoleon Hill*

and measure your progress brings visibility to your achievements, provides motivation and gives you the ability the correct the course if needed.

Make sure you don't measure your progress against other people; others are traveling their own journeys, have their own resources, and face their own challenges. You need to focus on your own journey and make sure you are heading in the right direction. The pace of your progress is important but what truly matters is the direction in which you are heading.

PUTTING IT ALL TOGETHER

Progress must also be shared with people you trust—your friends and family members. These people will not only be your cheerleaders as you move forward with your journey, but they will also keep you honest and provide you feedback if you are going off track.

As humans, we are programmed to choose immediate gratification over potential future benefits. So the only way to succeed is to fall in love with the process. The trick here is to first evolve our reductionist goals such as "lose 10 pounds" to holistic and inspiring visions such as "achieve optimal health", and then actually fall in love with the process of exercising and eating healthy, every day. If we keep seeing exercise and eating healthy as a boring

> "The characteristic of a genuine heroism is its persistency. All men have wandering impulses, fits and starts of generosity. But when you have resolved to be great, abide by yourself, and do not weakly try to reconcile yourself with the world. The heroic cannot be the common, nor the common the heroic."
>
> — *Ralph Waldo Emerson*

PUTTING IT ALL TOGETHER

inconvenience that we must do to achieve our goal, we will fall short. Our willpower will not take us too far. Falling in love with exercise and healthy food is the only way to achieve optimal health. Fall in love with the journey and enjoy the ride; the destination will be taken care of.

To summarize, if your dream is to be actualized, you must clarify it, align it with your values, write it down, feel it, share it with your dream team — a team of people who are stakeholders in your dream — and make it the central focus of everything that you think or do. Once you do that, you will:

- Start noticing the relevant, helpful things that you had never noticed before.

- Find that the right people will start showing up out of nowhere.

- Start moving away from people and activities that don't help you move toward your dreams.

- Start being aware of the non-essentials — activities that don't help you move toward your dream — and start eliminating them from your schedule.

PUTTING IT ALL TOGETHER

- Start living in the present moment by being fully mindful of the fact that what is in front of you is the most important thing/person in the world.

- Start loving the journey to a degree that destination becomes secondary.

What is being offered here is a broad architecture for you to build your own system based on where you are, where you want to go, and how you plan to get there? Your success in achieving your dreams through this system will be based on your own definition of success. A borrowed definition of success will lack the passion and the commitment needed to keep pushing when the going gets tough. Success is only real when it's discovered, defined, and experienced by *you*; anything else is just social conditioning and indoctrination. Even the ideas of morality and virtue are valid only when they help you become what you ought to be; otherwise, they are just tools meant to subjugate you. True happiness can only be achieved by realizing your true nature, by living your own values, and by achieving your version of success. Remember, it all starts with self-awareness — your *own* sense of who

PUTTING IT ALL TOGETHER

you are, what your strengths and weakness are, and what your dreams are.

Unfortunately, many people's understanding of themselves—who they are, and what they ought to be doing with their lives—is a concept borrowed from others, people who themselves are clueless about their own self. The key is to live your own conception of yourself. You are not what you are being told; you are what you choose to be. Rise out of the socially conditioned concept of yourself. Imagine a new future for yourself and have the courage to pursue it.

Don't just be an actor, be a writer, director, and producer of the movie of your life. You must find your own identity before you can improve it and ultimately transcend it.

Individuation is the ultimate freedom. You must exercise it!

Final Thoughts

FINAL THOUGHTS

"The Master…simply reminds people who they have always been."

— *Lao-Tzu*

If you have been with me so far on this journey, congratulations for staying focused! Because the data suggests that only 10% of the people who buy non-fiction books actually read them.

Here is the summary of what we have we learned:

- Success is a choice, not a chance.

FINAL THOUGHTS

- The way you are born and bred influences your personality, but you can change your destiny by choosing to harness the power of radical focus.

- You become what you focus on.

- Focusing on what matters is the only way to avoid the distraction of what is irrelevant.

- Goals are not enough; success requires a system.

- Focusology is a simple and holistic system to achieve real success in any aspect of life. This system has three modules:

    a. Macro Focus (Why): intention, vision, dream

    b. Micro Focus (What): action, daily routines, habits

    c. Nano Focus (How): attention, mindfulness, being in the present moment

- Willpower is limited; falling in love with the process — daily routines and habits needed to achieve the dreams — is the best way to make

FINAL THOUGHTS

  the desired change stick.

- Learning and continuously refining your system will enormously increase your chances of being, doing and achieving what truly matters in life.

The true joy of life can only be found in knowing what is meaningful and what can be controlled, and then bringing optimal focus to making it happen. Suffering and unhappiness, on the other hand, result from not knowing what is meaningful and what can be controlled, and then working hard to achieve it.

Knowledge is good, and learning is the foundation for any behavioral change. Knowledge has the potential to create thoughtful awareness; however, thoughtful awareness must evolve into thoughtless awareness for the experience to be fully optimized. You must build habits and automate desired behaviors.

A finger that points to the moon is not the moon; it's just a reflective endeavor; true change comes from experiencing the beauty of the moon…first hand. Commit to making lasting change by optimizing your habits and be ready to experience the beauty of

FINAL THOUGHTS

focus, because…

Focus is life!

And success is not a destination, it's a direction, so keep moving!

Index

Buddha, 118, 119

Commitment, 45, 46, 63, 89, 126, 153

Connect, 73

Connection, 43

Core Values, 81, 82

Dhyan, 119

Dream Board, 76

DREAM System, 144, 145, 146, 164

Experience, 143

Focus, 138, 139

Focusology, 4, 16, 18, 25, 32, 33, 34, 42, 145, 157, 164

Framework, 145

Goals, 24, 30, 51, 144, 151

Habits, 15, 23, 25, 27, 28, 33, 87, 88, 101, 106, 149, 157, 158

Hallucination, 28

Happiness, 44, 82

Karma, 22

Kismet, 22

Knowledge, 82, 149, 158

Ladder of Choice, 164

Listening, 66, 122, 136

love, 143

Macro Focus, 25, 26, 27, 30, 42, 44, 45, 46, 48, 49, 50, 51, 52, 54, 55, 57, 59, 63, 74, 76, 78, 86, 87, 91, 108, 147, 157

Manifestation, 60

FOCUSOLOGY

Micro Focus, 25, 26, 27, 30, 86, 87, 89, 91, 92, 132, 148, 157

Mindfulness, 16, 25, 119, 121, 123, 157

Mindset, 14, 15, 32, 50, 62, 67, 99, 122

Miracle, 122

Nano Focus, 25, 28, 31, 117, 118, 120, 121, 123, 125, 126, 128, 129, 134, 157

Nirvana, 38

Personality Assessment, 148

Placebo Effect, 65

Potential, 34, 36, 37, 38, 40, 43, 44, 56, 60, 65, 67, 93, 133, 151

Psychology, 144

Psychometric, 61, 62, 148

Rumi, 122

Self-awareness, 36, 63

Self-realization, 38

Self-transcendence, 37

Suffering, 158

System, 15, 18, 22, 24, 25, 28, 32, 34, 35, 42, 100, 144, 150, 153, 157, 158, 164

True North, 26

Universe, 31, 32, 94

Wheel of Life, 73

Acknowledgements

I would like to take this opportunity to express my profound gratitude to all those who helped shape the ideas and experiences that are expressed in this book. I'm especially indebted to those who encouraged and supported me through the process of putting these ideas and experiences in the form of this book. It is a long list that includes my family members, friends, advisors, and colleagues. I am tremendously grateful for their encouragement, support, and guidance.

Author

Mazhar Mansoor is a social scientist, management consultant, writer, and educator with over two decades of experience in areas such as strategic planning, performance management, training, and organizational development. He holds multiple graduate and post graduate degrees in management and social sciences.

Synthesizing insights from various academic disciplines, and experiences from various industries, Mr. Mansoor's work simplifies complex individual, social, and business challenges to develop and implement holistic, simple, and effective solutions.

Mr. Mansoor lives in Maryland and can be reached at:

focusology@outlook.com

Photos Attribution

Photos and graphics, including the cover photos, used in this book have been acquired from CanStockPhoto and other sources with proper permissions.

However, the following illustrations are original creations and are part of the Focusology system.

- Focusology
- Optimal Results
- Ladder of Choice
- The DREAM System
- Pyramid of Potential

Other Selected Books by the Author

FOCUSOLOGY

Optimal Xperience & Art of the FOCUS Method

A Breakthrough Personal Development Approach That Will Change Your Life Forever!

Paperback: 270 pages
Language: English
ISBN-10: 1493755420
ISBN-13: 978-1493755424
Product Dimensions: 5.5 x 0.7 x 8.5 inches
Link: https://tinyurl.com/OptimalXP

FOCUSOLOGY

The Philosophy of Optimal Leadership

Ideas, Inspiration, and Tools for the Current and Future Leaders.

Paperback: 198 pages
Language: English
ISBN-10: 0996175407
ISBN-13: 978-0996175401
Product Dimensions: 5.5 x 0.5 x 8.5 inches
Link: https://tinyurl.com/OptimalLeadership

www.ingramcontent.com/pod-product-compliance
Lightning Source LLC
Chambersburg PA
CBHW031354040426
42444CB00005B/283